Fair Trial

BICENTENNIAL ESSAYS ON THE BILL OF RIGHTS
Co-sponsored by Oxford University Press
and the Organization of American Historians

Kermit L. Hall, General Editor

EDITORIAL BOARD

Michal Belknap, Harold M. Hyman,
R. Kent Newmyer, William M. Wiecek

FAIR TRIAL
Rights of the Accused in American History
David J. Bodenhamer

THE GUARDIAN OF EVERY OTHER RIGHT
A Constitutional History of Property Rights
James W. Ely, Jr.

THE SHAPING OF THE FIRST AMENDMENT
1791 to the Present
Paul L. Murphy

PROMISES TO KEEP
*African Americans and the Constitutional
Order, 1776 to the Present*
Donald G. Nieman

Other Volumes Are in Preparation

FAIR
TRIAL

Rights of the Accused
in American History

DAVID J. BODENHAMER

New York   Oxford
OXFORD UNIVERSITY PRESS
1992

Oxford University Press

Oxford   New York   Toronto
Delhi   Bombay   Calcutta   Madras   Karachi
Petaling Jaya   Singapore   Hong Kong   Tokyo
Nairobi   Dar es Salaam   Cape Town
Melbourne   Auckland

and associated companies in
Berlin   Ibadan

Copyright © 1992 by Oxford University Press, Inc.

Published by Oxford University Press, Inc.
200 Madison Avenue, New York, New York 10016

Oxford is a registered trademark of Oxford University Press

All rights reserved. No part of this publication may be reproduced,
stored in a retrieval system, or transmitted, in any form or by any means,
electronic, mechanical, photocopying, recording, or otherwise,
without the prior permission of Oxford University Press.

Library of Congress Cataloging-in-Publication Data
Bodenhamer, David J.
Fair trial : rights of the accused in American history /
David J. Bodenhamer.
p.   cm.
(Bicentennial essays on the Bill of Rights)
Includes bibliographical references and index.
ISBN 0-19-505558-6 — ISBN 0-19-505559-4 (pbk.)
1. Due process of law—United States—History.
2. Fair trial—United States—History.
3. Criminal procedure—United States—History.
I. Title.   II. Series.
KF4765.B63   1992   347.73'05—dc20   [347.3075]   90-19611

2 4 6 8 9 7 5 3 1
Printed in the United States of America
on acid-free paper

To my Mother and the memory of my Father

Editor's Preface

This book is part of the Bicentennial Essays on the Bill of Rights, a series that has resulted from the fruitful collaboration of the Organization of American Historians' Committee on the Bicentennial of the Constitution and Oxford University Press. The committee in 1986 concluded that one of the most appropriate ways in which historians could commemorate the then forthcoming bicentennial of the Bill of Rights was to foster better teaching about it in undergraduate classrooms. Too often, the committee decided, students could have learned more about the history of liberty in America if they would only have had basic texts analyzing the evolution of the most important provisions of the Bill of Rights. There are, of course, many fine specialized studies of the first ten amendments to the Constitution, but these works invariably concentrate on a particular Supreme Court case and technical legal developments. What the committee wanted, and what Nancy Lane at Oxford University Press vigorously supported, were books that would explore in brief compass the main themes in the evolution of civil liberties and civil rights as they have been revealed through the Bill of Rights. The books in this series, therefore, bridge a significant gap in the literature of the history of liberty by offering synthetic examinations rooted in the best and most recent literature in history, political science, and law. Their authors have, as well, framed these nontechnical studies within the contours of American history. The authors have taken as their goal making the history of rights and liberties resonate with developments in the nation's social, cultural, and political history.

Kermit L. Hall

Preface

Fair Trial is a work of synthesis and interpretation. It is an attempt to guide general readers and students through the vast, unintegrated, sometimes obscure, and often arcane literature on rights of the accused in American history. The book is also an effort to trace the course of legal change and relate it to developments in the broader society. My focus is on defendants' rights in theory and practice, in local, state, and national courts and in any other forum where the language of rights entered a political, legal, and social dialogue. My aim is to promote understanding of these rights and their central importance to the meaning of American liberty.

I have looked forward with great anticipation to the day when I could thank publicly those individuals who have made this work possible. Only cynics will conclude that my joy stems from the knowledge that this Preface ends my creative labor on this manuscript.

My greatest intellectual debt is to all scholars who have written on rights of the accused. Any misinterpretation of their work is my fault alone, but without them *Fair Trial* certainly would be an impoverished, unenlightened, and uninspired effort. The Bibliography recognizes those individuals whose work I have found most useful.

I also owe much to friends who have supported my work. My former colleagues in the Department of History at the University of Southern Mississippi offered personal encouragement and a professionally supportive environment during all twelve years of our relationship, as did my associates in the university's administration. I am especially grateful for time off during the fall semester of 1988, my last months at USM, which allowed me to write the first three chapters. My current colleagues in the

Department of History, the POLIS Research Center, and the School of Liberal Arts at Indiana University–Purdue University at Indianapolis also deserve thanks for their patience and understanding.

Several individuals have done yeoman's duty in reading this manuscript and offering suggestions that invariably improved its content and style. James W. Ely, Jr., read every chapter promptly and offered sage advice, even though he too was deep into the writing of his own companion volume for this series. Harold Hyman and Michal Belknap provided valuable guidance as members of the editorial advisory board, as did Kent Newmyer for Chapters 1 and 2. David Koenig critiqued the first several chapters at my request and saved me from serious errors of fact and interpretation. Maxwell Bloomfield commented upon Chapter 3 when I presented it as a paper at the Society for Historians of the Early Republic. Kermit Hall proved to be a splendid general editor. Regrettably, I can blame errors on no one but myself.

The support of friends and colleagues is important in writing a book, but it is the encouragement of family that makes the enterprise enjoyable and worthwhile. Karen, Jeff, and Jace (and Poof, they constantly reminded me) kept me in touch with the pleasures of their worlds and tolerated me as I struggled with the challenges of mine. As always, Penny offered her incomparable gifts of friendship and love.

The dedication acknowledges the debt of a lifetime.

Indianapolis   D. J. B.
January 1991

Contents

Fair Trial

INTRODUCTION

In a New York City subway station on June 28, 1972, John Skagen, a white off-duty policeman, stopped James Richardson, a black man on his way to work, identified himself, and ordered Richardson against a wall with his hands up. Richardson complied. Skagen began a search; suddenly Richardson drew a snub-nosed .32 caliber revolver from under his waist-length dashiki. The men exchanged shots. Skagen staggered backwards with two bullets in his shoulder while a slightly wounded Richardson fled up the stairs toward the street. Skagen recovered and gave chase. Reaching the bottom of the stairs, he raised his gun and fired a single shot, hitting Richardson in the shoulder. At the top of the stairs a uniformed policeman appeared. Not recognizing Skagen, he drew his revolver and emptied it at the man Richardson identified as his assailant. Skagen fell, mortally wounded.

After his capture, Richardson confessed to shooting a policeman while fleeing arrest. On July 12, less than one month after the shooting, a grand jury indicted him for capital murder. Two years later, a trial jury convicted Richardson of manslaughter and two minor charges. He received an eight-year sentence in the state penitentiary.[1]

Few crimes in America stir more public response than the killing of a policeman. Such cases are richly symbolic of popular attitudes. A policeman represents law and order; the accused, a threat to stability. Tragically, these images carry greater emotional power when the slain officer is white and the suspect is black. The death of John Skagen, coming as it did after the racial and political turmoil of the late 1960s, offered authorities good opportunity to slight the procedures that in theory define a fair trial. No official sought this option. James Richardson received all the rights guaranteed to defendants under the U. S. Constitu-

3

tion: protection against self-incrimination while in custody (the so-called *Miranda* warning), indictment by a grand jury, representation by counsel, and trial by jury, among others.

Ironically, some of the actions taken by both prosecution and defense in the case served to defeat the provisions of the Bill of Rights. The trial did not occur until the fall of 1974, over two years after the shooting. Such a delay is hard to reconcile with the Fifth Amendment's guarantee of a speedy trial, but the delay resulted from the petition of Richardson's lawyer for more time to prepare his defense. The prosecution attempted to secure a guilty plea in exchange for a lighter sentence, that is, it sought to "plea bargain" in an effort to avoid trial, an action hardly reflective of the Constitution's requirement of a public trial.

These elements of *People* v. *Richardson* suggest potential conflict between two legitimate ends—the requirements of fairness and the need to maintain order through swift and certain punishment of wrongdoing. The case facts also caution against any attempt to place right or justice exclusively on the side of the state or defendant. The history of rights of the accused is not so neat or simple. But it is important to understand this story because it is central to what Americans consider their unique constitutional liberty.

"The history of American freedom is, in no small measure, the history of procedure."[2] Justice Felix Frankfurter's telling epigraph expresses a fundamental article of faith about our constitutional heritage: liberty and rights cannot exist without due process of law. Procedural fairness and consistency are essential elements of due process, a concept that has long been the touchstone of Anglo-American jurisprudence. Although lacking precise definition, jurists have given two meanings to the phrase— procedural due process or the insistence on predetermined rules to try cases, and substantive due process or the requirement that these rules be reasonable. But no one hàs challenged Justice Robert Jackson's claim that whatever else due process might mean, procedural fairness "is what it most uncompromisingly requires."[3]

In the criminal law of a free society, a proper concern for due process is crucial. Without it, individual liberty is especially vulnerable to arbitrary governmental power. And, as legal historian Zechariah Chafee, Jr., has noted, freedom from official capriciousness is essential to all other human rights.[4] This ideal is an old one, and its significance in western thought can scarcely be overstated. Government holds enormous power.

Not only does it possess the resources to monitor personal actions but it alone has the legitimate authority to accuse, prosecute, and punish individuals. Thus, any criminal trial between the government and a citizen is inherently unequal. Our conception of justice demands that this inequality be redressed. Anglo-American law balances the contest between government and the individual by restraining official power. It makes defendants' rights inviolable and concedes that abridgement of these rights will result in accquittal.

The federal Bill of Rights devotes more attention to the requirements for a fair criminal process than it does to any other right or group of rights. Amendments 4, 5, 6, and 8 outline seventeen provisions regarding trial and punishment that constitute a miniature code of criminal procedure. The amendments seek to protect the accused from unreasonable searches and seizures, double jeopardy, and self-incrimination as well as to guarantee defendants a public jury trial, representation by counsel, and the right to confront prosecution witnesses. Equally important is the Fifth Amendment's injunction (and the similar one of its lineal descendant, the Fourteenth Amendment) that no one shall be deprived of life or liberty without due process of law.

Not all rights important to our conception of justice are found in the Bill of Rights. Habeas corpus, the so-called Great Writ that requires a judge to release an unlawfully detained prisoner, is listed in Article I, Section IX of the Constitution as a privilege that Congress cannot suspend under normal circumstances. An absolute prohibition of bills of attainder and *ex post facto* measures resides in the same section. These clauses require laws to operate generally and not against particular people and not to make new crimes out of conduct that has already occurred. Article III secures a jury trial in all federal criminal cases. State constitutions and statutes also contain provisions that balance the contest between government and the accused. Although in theory controlling only state and local officials, these rules parallel the fundamental rights protected under the due process clauses of the Fifth and Fourteenth Amendments.

Several problems confront anyone who seeks to understand the Bill of Rights' standards of due process for criminal defendants. One is the broad scope of the topic. Few social and political interests remain untouched by these rights because criminal process, as nineteenth-century commentator Joel P. Bishop noted, "sustains a more intimate relation to the everyday life of every member of the community than any other division of law."[5] Not everyone will own property or make a contract, but each person falls under the command of the criminal code. Criminal justice also brings into sharp focus the precarious balance between the power of the state and the freedom of the individual. As a result, it involves "the most insistent and fundamental social interests."[6]

Another problem lies in the nature of the amendments themselves. Drafted by eighteenth-century revolutionaries to protect individuals from arbitrary action by the central government, the Bill of Rights now is viewed as an equally powerful restraint on state and local authorities. The application of these rights to all levels of government is a product of the last fifty years. Yet the rights did not lie fallow or untended during the century and a half between the adoption of the Constitution and the modern era. Nor did they suddenly emerge during the Revolution as newly invented rights of Americans. The framers based these guarantees on colonial practices and on their understanding of English history, especially the long tradition of restricting the power of government. In fact, a fear of power persuaded revolutionary leaders to make the rights part of their state constitutions. The Constitution's pronouncement of rights was a political afterthought. Under the federal system, states, not the national government, had the initial responsibility for protecting these rights. As a result, many of the meanings we attach to due process first found expression in numerous state and local courts and in state legislative actions.

Criminal process also has shaped the development of defendants' rights. The legal system operates only when a party with a legitimate interest (or standing) demands that a court with proper jurisdiction hear a dispute or punish a crime.[7] Courts do not consider hypothetical issues. Constitutional rights receive voice only in real cases. This circumstance, combined with the personal harm or property loss involved in criminal trials, makes it difficult at times for victims and society to acknowledge a defendant's rights. Further, the legal system is adversarial in its operation. Each side to a dispute or conflict has the obligation to present evidence that will prove its claim and rebut contradictory evidence offered by the other side. In criminal matters, the defendant enters the trial with a presumption of innocence that the prosecution must overcome. But this presumption is often an abstraction that may not correspond to community sentiment, especially when the suspect is poor or a member of a racial or ethnic minority.

Rights of the accused have developed in response to social and political change. The guarantees contained in the Bill of Rights are not static, nor have their meanings been certain and fixed since the 1790s. Even seemingly straightforward requirements such as the right to jury trial, not to mention more general prescriptions of what constitutes due process, have been subject to much dispute.

Capital punishment offers the most dramatic example of the impact social attitudes have on constitutional meanings. At the time of its adoption, the Eighth Amendment's prohibition of cruel and unusual punishment did not remove death as an acceptable sentence. Executions were permissible punishments under the criminal laws of every state in the new republic. There was no consensus on which punishments were cruel and unusual. Two centuries later the debate continues, although with more certain boundaries of what is unconstitutional. By common agreement, we no longer permit public executions. Under court decisions, death can be inflicted only under carefully and elaborately drawn procedures. The amendment reads the same as it did in 1791. But social attitudes have changed, and so too has our understanding of what the Constitution requires. In less visible fashion, the same theme explains the development of other rights of the accused.

There is yet another important interpretative guide for understanding constitutional guarantees of due process. Former Speaker of the U. S. House of Representatives Thomas P. ''Tip'' O'Neill liked to remind his colleagues that all politics are local. This observation is equally true of justice, both in its procedures and its substance. American criminal justice has been characterized by decentralization and discretion. In matters of arrest, trial, and punishment, popularly elected local officials decide what actions to take in regard to the accused. Through various means—for example, grand and petit juries, locally elected sheriffs, prosecutors, and judges, and so on—the American legal system reflects community norms or popular judgment to a degree unparalleled among other western nations.

The administration of criminal justice, notes Professor David Fellman, ''depends upon the temper of the community, the nature of its prejudices and values, the character of its scapegoats, the state of the economy, the quality of its bench and bar, its educational system, and related nonlegal factors.''[8] Prosecutors choose not to try certain crimes, believing that the offense does not violate community standards. Sheriffs more readily arrest some suspects because of racial, ethnic, or class prejudices. Such a large grant of discretion, inevitable in any system of criminal justice but heightened in its effect by the decentralization of American life, means that the reality of constitutional guarantees often fall short of the ideal. It also means that justice has frequently, perhaps inevitably, been measured by local standards.

We accept the idea (if not the practice) of local standards and individual treatment because it comports with popular notions of justice, even though it may contradict expressed beliefs in equality and universal norms of due process. Until the mid-twentieth century American law avoided this potential conflict by trusting local and state officials to safeguard constitutional protections of defendants' rights. Only when social and political change dictated a national policy in this and other areas did due process find a place on the agenda of federal judges. But because of the long-standing deference to local authority the nationalization of due process did not proceed swiftly or without controversy.

This book traces the legal and constitutional history of rights of the accused. Several developments provide the framework for this story—among them, the English tradition of rights, the revolutionary heritage, nineteenth-century democratic individualism, the transition from a rural-agrarian to an urban-industrial society, the changing nature and meaning of community, the impact of professionalization and bureaucratization, and the rise of judicial activism. It is not possible to develop a comprehensive analysis of each guarantee contained in the Bill of Rights, nor is it necessary. Different rights received greater attention during various periods in American history. For instance, the antebellum decades witnessed vigorous debates on the nature of indictments, the role, composition, and qualification of grand and petit juries, and the form and legitimacy of criminal punishment. Delays in trial or inadequacies of counsel were not issues of major concern until the twentieth century.

Much of the narrative focus in the first half of this essay will be upon the states, not the central government. Until the middle of this century, matters of criminal law, including constitutional protections of defendants' rights, remained the prerogative of state and local governments, with occasional oversight and intervention by federal agencies. As a result, this book necessarily devotes attention to the understanding of defendants' rights as manifested in state courts and legislatures. Such focus does not ignore the development of federal guarantees because the Bill of Rights echoed, with few exceptions, the provisions of earlier state charters. So it is appropriate for the first half of the book to concentrate on state and local criminal process and leave to the last half the nationalization of these guarantees. Finally, constitutional rights here are defined generically and as interpreted by numerous governmental and extralegal agencies. American law occupies a greater province than what is contained in the opinions of the U. S. Supreme Court.

What emerges from the history of defendants' rights is a heightened respect for the maxim that American government is one of laws, not of people. To be certain, there are numerous examples that challenge the truthfulness of this sentiment, but more often we can rightly admire how consistent has been the expression of this ideal and how powerful has been its hold on the American mind. This book is no paean to the Bill of Rights. The document does not need one. Its importance in our common lives is sufficient testimony to its value and to the success of the framers' great experiment in liberty.

1

THE COLONIAL
BACKGROUND

Conflicting images have shaped popular and even scholarly conceptions of colonial justice. Draconian punishments, symbolized by the gibbet, stocks, and whipping post, were hallmarks of the legal system, although in practice law enforcement was lax. Rights were few, but the consensual and largely peaceful nature of early settlements made them unnecessary. Colonists were more intent on subduing nature and the Indians than on threatening the lives or property of their fellow citizens. Legal procedure was simple and often applied without great attention to formality, a condition that fit the sparsely settled continent. The sources of law were the Bible (especially the Deuteronomic catalog of wrongdoings and punishments), the remembered customs of local manorial practice, and to a lesser extent the English common law. But the limited knowledge of unsophisticated lawyers—where they existed at all—made the administration of justice simple and community vigilance kept violations few.

Certain incidents appear to support this picture of colonial law. Witness the tragic case of Thomas Granger, told in the diary of William Bradford, governor of Plymouth Plantation. Granger was an adolescent servant living apart from his parents when "he was this year [1642] detected of buggery, and indicted for the same, with a mare, a cow, two goats, five sheep, two calves, and a turkey." Upon examination, Granger confessed in private to the magistrates—"though at first he strived to deny it"—and he repeated his confession publicly, first to ministers and later to the court and jury. A strange proceeding followed, whereby Granger had to separate the offending animals from the rest of the herd: "he declared which were they and which were not." The reason for this practice soon becomes clear. "A very sad spectacle it was," Bradford writes. "For first the mare and then the cow and the rest of the lesser cattle were killed before his face, according to the law, Leviticus xx.15; and then he himself was executed. The cattle were all cast into a great and large pit that was digged of purpose for them, and no use made of any part of them."[1]

At first glance, the matter of Thomas Granger epitomizes the traditional view of criminal justice in colonial America. Officials evidently pressured young Granger to confess, he lacked counsel, and biblical law defined his crime and punishment. These items so correspond to prevailing notions that it is easy to overlook significant elements which do not meet expectations. The magistrates accorded the servant at least some of the procedural safeguards that defined a fair trial for Englishmen in the seventeenth century. An indictment provided knowledge of the charges against him, and he had a speedy and public jury trial. Although the record is sparse, there is no reason to conclude that the colony denied Granger any rights that defendants had in England. Modern minds may shrink at the harshness of the sentence, but by the standards of his day Thomas Granger apparently received a fair trial. Not only was this an Englishman's right, it was what made the common law the most envied in the western world.

The development of English criminal justice already had a long and complex history by the seventeenth century. Its roots extended to the period preceding the Norman Conquest (1066). In Anglo-Saxon England criminal proceedings were oral, personal, accusatory, and local. One person publicly charged another before the community, which in turn decided what form of proof—compurgation, ordeal, or battle—the trial should take. Compurgation, or oath-taking, consisted of swearing a sacred pledge to the truthfulness of one's claim or denial, supported by similar oaths from community members. Ordeal, usually reserved for more serious crimes, required a physical trial to test a plea. The accused's arm might be immersed in boiling water or branded with a hot iron, with the manner and swiftness of healing carefully noted as a divine sign of guilt or innocence. Verdicts for the gravest crimes were secured by battle, a physical contest between accuser and accused whereby God would lend strength to the cause of the truthful party. Whichever method was chosen, certain features of this primitive system would become hallmarks of English justice. There was a definite and known accuser who publicly confronted his antagonist, trials were open, and judges acted as arbiters to enforce the rules of fairness.

The arrival of William the Conqueror introduced a new type of criminal process, the continental system of inquest, to England. A royal official summoned a body of men from the same neighborhood to reply under oath to any question that might be addressed to them. This was the inquest.[2] Used first to determine property ownership for purposes of tax assessment, the process evolved into the grand jury of accusation under King Henry II (1154–89). The Assizes of Clarendon (1166) and North-hampton (1176) provided that twelve free men from every hundred of the county would submit to the King's justices all the crimes they knew of or had heard about. This new method of criminal proceeding retained the character of accusatorial justice but challenged and ultimately supplanted the older forms of proof. When the church banned clergy from administering the ordeals in 1215, no practical way remained to try individuals charged by the grand jury. Using the jury of presentment or accusation to resolve questions of guilt was unacceptable, so a separate petit (petty) or trial jury of twelve local men emerged to determine truth.

By the mid-fifteenth century, the new procedures were in common use. Accusation by one neighborhood body initiated the criminal process, followed by trial before a second body of the community. The changes retained some features of the pre-Norman accusatorial methods—a prisoner knew the charges and confronted his opponents in open court—and added elements from the inquest—the defendant had the freedom to challenge prosecution witnesses, to offer his own explanations, and to have his fate determined by his peers. Unquestionably, he faced certain disadvantages, among them lack of counsel and inability to summon defense witnesses, but "the trial was supremely fair, judged by any standard known in the western world of that day."[3]

The contrast between English procedure and developing continental practice was dramatic. In the same year as the Magna Carta, 1215, the Fourth Lateran Council in Rome charted a new course for criminal justice. The reforms of Pope Innocent III (1198–1216)—which also banned the clergy from trial by ordeal—transformed canon or church law into an inquisitorial system in order to protect the faith from heretics. There were few parallels with the English inquest. Accusations were often made in secret, and the judge was also the prosecutor. At the heart of the process was a self-incriminating oath required of all suspects. The oath ex officio permitted judges to obtain statements from the defendant that could later be used as a basis for formal criminal proceedings against him. Refusal to take the oath justified torture to learn the truth. In theory applicable only to church trials for heresy, the inquisition became the model for the civil law jurisdictions of Europe. "Everywhere the secret examination, the inquisitional oath, and torture became the standard, at first used only in 'extraordinary' cases but quickly degenerating into a completely routine procedure for all cases but the most petty."[4]

Different attitudes toward the defendant symbolized the separate goals of continental and English law. In Europe criminal process focused on securing the guilt of the accused. There were rules of evidence to protect the person wrongly accused, but better that the innocent should suffer than the guilty escape. Conversely, the maxim of English justice remained what Chief Justice John Fortescue first expressed in the mid-fifteenth century: "Indeed, one would much rather that twenty guilty persons should escape the punishment of death, than that one innocent person should be condemned, and suffer capitally."[5]

Yet not everything was right in English law, nor was everyone pleased with its evolving structure or practice. Tudor and Stuart monarchs created new prerogative courts in the late sixteenth and early seventeenth centuries that acted outside the constraints of common law. Star Chamber, the judicial arm of the Privy Council, the primary council of state, became notorious for the use of inquisitorial tactics against opponents of the crown. Secret proceedings and torture were mainstays of this court, although neither practice was permitted under common law. As an extraordinary power to be imposed only when state security was at issue, the efficiency of torture in securing convictions soon prompted its use in less serious cases.

Another unwelcome innovation was the preliminary examination of accused persons. Parliamentary statutes in the 1550s required justices of the peace to interrogate all persons suspected of crime and their accusers. Not only did this step diminish the role of the grand jury, it promoted efficiency as a central goal of criminal justice. Examinations were held in secret, testimony against the accused was revealed only at trial, and any damaging admissions by the suspect were fair evidence against him. The influence of common law was not lost completely, however. The trial was public, the accused could retract or deny any confession (he was never under oath), the judge remained neutral, and the jury's verdict was unimpeachable. Even so, the new procedures introduced features many Englishmen considered odius to their system of justice.

Equally vexing were the complicated maze of local, county, and royal courts and the obscure and often mysterious language of criminal law. The creation of new courts rarely eliminated old ones; it simply added a new layer of tribunals to an already cumbersome system. Assize and quarter session courts handled most criminal matters, although borough and leet courts, both vestiges of the manorial period, maintained some authority over misdemeanors. Moral violations could also bring offenders before ecclesiastical or church courts. Further, a jumble of statutes and precedents kept the common law of crime unknowable to most people. Written in law Latin and French, much of it was beyond the ken of all but an educated few. This condition may have enhanced the law's function as an instrument of social control, but it left many Englishmen dissatisfied with the law and uncertain of their rights.

Dissatisfaction with criminal justice accompanied the first English settlers to the new world. The law was too bloody, exacting death as an atonement for even trivial crimes. At the assizes, judges resorted to the hangman's noose and preached sermons on legal vengeance to the propertyless and uneducated. The law was also capricious. Until 1547 murderers who could read escaped the gallows by invoking the ancient privilege known as benefit of clergy, while otherwise decent men died for stealing bread so their children might eat. And the law set traps for people in the form of church courts that prosecuted men and women for acts perceived to be immoral. Perhaps the most disturbing problem was widespread corruption, revealed by frequent occurrences of contempt, perjury, and jury-tampering. These actions mocked the common law's reputation for fairness.[6]

Demands for reform were not lost on migrating Englishmen. They too blamed an archaic and capricious legal system for England's corrupt, crime-ridden society. But reform was possible. Colonial charters required only that laws be consistent with English practice. Settlers would be free to create rational laws that clearly defined expected behavior and provided a simplified court structure. The first American lawmakers, remarks one scholar, had "the freedom of chancellors and the power of judges."[7] Enhancing this authority was the scarcity of law books and the paucity of men trained in law. The absence of lawyers, in particular, invited experimentation with legal forms.

If the new world provided an opportunity to reform the law, change did not occur for its own sake. Colonists did not abandon their past or forget their experience simply because they were on a separate continent. An analysis of early colonial law reveals that lawmakers followed traditional practice when they judged it rational and just. Their major goal was to simplify the law, removing its obscure and contradictory provisions and making it knowable. In this aim, they largely succeeded. They restated the law in English and published it for widespread distribution, often requiring that it be read before certain public gatherings.

Colonists deviated from English law primarily to mitigate its harshness. This policy of leniency did not change the definition of crime or remove death as a punishment; it did permit other sanctions, however, thus providing judges with an alternative to more severe measures. The early Puritan colonies, for example, abolished capital punishment for any form of theft. English law in the first half of the sixteenth century was far bloodier, with over 200 crimes mandating this penalty, most of them offenses against property. Moral and material considerations influenced the change. Radical Protestants, including the Puritans, valued all life as sacred and would not take it without divine sanction. More earthly colonists recognized the shortage of labor and wanted to do nothing to diminish its supply.[8]

Reform of the criminal law did not end with changes in the number and definition of crimes or the severity of punishment. Rights of the accused also became an important part of colonial codes. Unlike the common law, which buried these safeguards in the great mass of precedent, colonial laws gave them prominent attention. Indeed, many colonial statutes evince a higher regard for the rights of individuals than did contemporary English law.[9] The codes explained in plain terms what the rights were and what purposes they served.

The Massachusetts Body of Liberties symbolizes the extent to which lawmakers embraced advanced statements on individual rights. The company of Puritans that settled Massachusetts Bay in 1630 initially established an oligarchical government to protect the sanctity of the City on the Hill. Although the colony's leaders resisted popular government, the people, Governor John Winthrop wrote in his journal, "thought their condition very unsafe while so much power rested in the discretion of magistrates." A major objective of the colonists was the framing of "a body . . . of laws, in resemblance to a Magna Carta." Adopted in

1641, the Body of Liberties blended common law and Puritan theology. Its expressed purpose was to ensure the "tranquillitie and Stabilitie of Churches and Commonwealths" by recognizing the "free fruition of such liberties Immunities and priveledges as humanitie, Civilitie, and Christianitie call for as due to every man in his place and proportion without impeachment and Infringement." The "deniall or deprivall thereof," the preamble concluded, would mean the "disturbance if not the ruine of both [church and state]."[10]

The list of liberties was comprehensive for its day. Many of its specific guarantees anticipated the fundamental protections contained over a century later in the federal Bill of Rights. Especially prominent were numerous safeguards for the criminally accused: speedy and equal justice, bail, right of counsel, trial by jury (mentioned in six different sections), challenge of jurors, double jeopardy, cruel and unusual punishment, and prohibition of torture. These guarantees were not unabridged. Unlike today, there was no requirement for counsel. Also, assistance by counsel had to be for "noe fee or reward" and did not exempt the defendant from answering the demands of the court. Torture was permissible in capital cases in which conspiracy was suspected, although only after conviction of a principal on "cleare and suffitient evidence." Nor were these provisions new. Each of them had some precedent in common law, royal decree, or parliamentary statute. Still, they were stated positively in a written code, a circumstance unprecedented in English experience.

Other colonial documents offered similar positive expressions of fundamental rights. The Pennsylvania Frame of Government of 1682 declared itself a "charter of liberties," and in its second part, the "Laws Agreed upon in England," William Penn, the Quaker proprietor who had suffered religious prosecution in England, guaranteed open courts, proceedings conducted quickly and in English, copies of complaints delivered to defendants, indictment by grand jury, and trial by jury which "shall have final judgment." A new constitution, the famous Charter of Privileges of 1701, did not mention these guarantees but did provide that "all criminals shall have the same Privileges of Witnesses and Council as their Prosecutors." The West New Jersey proprietors went further, mandating jury trial in all cases and permitting accused persons to challenge thirty-five prospective jurors or more upon a valid reason. Even New York, one of the most conservative royal colonies, enacted laws which made absolute the right to bail except in cases of capital felony and treason and the right to grand and petty juries.[11]

Where did colonists get these ideas? Colonial charters reserved to migrating Englishmen, in the language of the Virginia Company's grant in 1606, "all Liberties, Franchises, and Immunities . . . to all intents and purposes, as if they had been abiding and born, within this our realm of England." But what were these rights? The charters did not define them, even in rudimentary form. The heralded documents upon which the English traditionally based their rights were also curiously uninformative about specific safeguards. Magna Carta, for example, established the basic principle that no man, even the king, was above the law, but its provisions disappointed anyone who sought a detailed listing of rights. Chapter 39, its most influential section, simply guaranteed the personal liberty of all freemen "except by the lawful judgment of peers or the law of the land."

The seventeenth-century struggle between Parliament and crown proved instructive for colonists, who interpreted their experiences with government in similar terms. At issue was the king's prerogative, especially his authority to circumscribe the rights of his subjects. Beginning with the Petition of Right in 1628 and proceeding through the Bill of Rights in 1689, parliamentary spokesmen argued the rule of law and established legislative supremacy as a principle of English constitutionalism. The colonists did not remain untouched by these debates. Various writings by political philosophers and participants to the conflict found a receptive audience in North America. Especially appealing were the reform platforms of the Levellers and other radical groups in the English Civil War (1642–60) that promised to lighten the punishments prescribed by law, to simplify criminal procedure, and to make rights certain by placing them in writing. Tracts, petitions, and treatises voiced a litany of rights, the supposed origin of which was the Magna Carta. In the 1620s, for instance, Sir Edward Coke, a leading legal commentator, saw the document as a guarantor of jury trial, an absolute prohibition on arbitrary arrest, and a pledge of full, free, and equal justice to all. Writers also explored what was included in the Charter's elusive phrase, "the law of the land," finding in it a breadth of language that served far wider purposes than the feudal barons intended.

But much of what Englishmen considered as rights was customary, that is, found in common law, not in statutes or state documents.

Sometimes, especially during early settlement, the colonists relied upon memory to identify procedural safeguards. Founders did not come to the new world armed with codes or legal materials, but neither were they ignorant about law and government. Numbers of them had been magistrates or lawyers in England and could draw on their personal knowledge of criminal process. Equally important were the recollections of ordinary settlers, many of whom doubtless had some prior acquaintance with English courts as participants or observers. Yet much custom was merely local and of limited value to provinces housing immigrants from different parts of England. With increasing frequency, lawmakers turned to commentators who had glossed the vast body of materials that constituted the common law.

Chief among these authorities was Sir Edward Coke, Chief Justice of King's Bench, a leading parliamentary antagonist of the Stuart monarchy, and author of several works on common law, the most important of which was the four-volume *Institutes of the Laws of England*. Coke venerated the common law and from his study drew the conclusion that its development had been continuous and progressive since the days of the Anglo-Saxons. Although uncritical and inaccurate, settlers who sought support for their claim to traditional rights found great solace in these works. In his *Second Institute*, for example, Coke set down a series of common law rights that protected the freeman's life and liberty, among them due process of law, habeas corpus, and imprisonment only for certain cause. The works of other commentators also influenced the elaboration of colonial law. Michael Dalton's handbook on the duties of justices of the peace, *Countrey Justice* (1619), did not embrace Coke's celebratory view of common law, but it provided lawmakers with the forms and procedures that were part of England's criminal process.[12]

Colonists also borrowed ideas about individual rights from each other. This process of imitation was perhaps inevitable because of the uncertainties of English law and because the colonists found themselves in similar circumstances as they sought to transfer their rights to the new world. Experience was the great teacher here. Colonists quickly discovered that they could not duplicate the mother country's legal system with exactness. Settlements were too scattered, distances too great, and men learned in the law too few. Colonial populations were ethnically diverse and mobile, unlike the homogeneous English. In such a society it became important to simplify the forms of government and mold them to the demands of a new environment. Charters of settlement did not allow wholesale revisions of the common law, but they permitted colonial legislatures to transfer law selectively and innovate where necessary. This lawmakers did. It is noteworthy that colonists used such discretion, in part, to advance defendants' rights.

By the eve of the Revolution safeguards for the accused had become part of a common language about the liberties of Englishmen who resided in the new world. Significantly, the colonial conception of due process was more extensive than its English counterpart and contrasted dramatically with the developing procedures of European states. In fact, there is a decidedly modern tint to these guarantees. A composite list of procedural rights guaranteed in colonial codes is surprisingly long:

1. No search or seizure without warrant.
2. Right to reasonable bail.
3. Confessions out of court invalid.
4. Right to have cause determined with reasonable speed.
5. Grand jury indictment in capital cases.
6. Right to know the charges.
7. Straightforward pleading with double jeopardy barred.
8. Right to challenge jurors.
9. Process to compel witnesses for the defense.
10. Right to confront accusers.
11. Trial by jury.
12. Limitation of punishment to the convict: no corruption of blood or forfeiture.
13. No cruel or unusual punishment.
14. Equal protection of the law: dependent classes—women, children, and servants—have access to the courts.
15. Equal execution of the law: no capricious mitigation or application of penalties.
16. [Limited] Right of appeal.[13]

These procedural guarantees existed on paper and in the rhetoric of legislators, but did they reflect colonial practice? To some degree, yes. Both representative government and a fluid social and political structure encouraged a close correspondence between lawmaking and the perceived needs or desires of the electorate. But it would be unrealistic to believe that legal expression of rights mirrored our own understanding or always found perfect voice in provincial courtrooms.

Even a brief examination of seventeenth- and eighteenth-century criminal justice abruptly dispels any notion that the rights of defendants embodied modern definitions in anything other than embryonic form. Although recognizable in outline and language, due process held a more circumscribed meaning for colonial Americans. In short, the phrase referred to the means for placing an issue before the courts and moving it to verdict—in other words, procedural due process. The exercise of criminal justice in New England and the Chesapeake, the two oldest and most populous areas of settlement, provides good instruction in understanding the practical meaning of rights accorded to criminal defendants.

Historians usually distinguish New England from the middle and southern colonies when discussing English settlements in the new world, and for good reason. Puritans intended their efforts to serve as models of righteousness for the reform of a corrupt mother country, while economic success was the overarching goal of colonists further south. Differences in the social and economic structures of the two societies were both apparent and real. Communalism, found in both congregation and township, typified the densely populated New England colonies. Separate existence was more common in the sparsely settled areas to the south. Merchants dominated the northern economies, planters the southern. Literate freemen composed the workforce of New England, while uneducated apprentice laborers and African slaves filled the manpower needs of the tobacco and rice cultures.

Differences among the colonies also existed in the sources and purpose of criminal law. Massachusetts, New Haven colony, and Connecticut derived a substantial portion of their law from the Bible, often reducing the number and severity of property crimes while converting frequently unprosecuted or lightly punished misdemeanors such as adultery and fornication into capital felonies. Although codes were harsh, the magistrates who administered justice in these northern colonies usually mitigated extreme punishments upon a sign of repentance. The purpose of law was to control sin and redeem the sinner, not destroy him. Virginia and Maryland, on the other hand, took their law overwhelmingly from English statutes and common law and followed English practice more closely in its administration. Serious property crimes were typically capital offenses, and, though hangings were not uncommon, local juries often convicted defendants on less serious charges. Control of uneducated and ill-tempered workers was more important to Chesapeake planters than the salvation of souls. Still, differences between the colonies should not be exaggerated. Even in Puritan societies most of the law came from English precedents. The New England colonies of Plymouth and Rhode Island, for instance, preferred English law, almost to the exclusion of Biblical commands. And the frontier environment made the preservation of order a necessity for any colony, whether northern or southern.[14]

Just as the law in books distinguished New England somewhat from its Chesapeake counterparts, so too did the law at work. Again, the differences were not large—both societies, after all, were English—but they reveal the range of applications permitted under the common law.[15]

The Puritan colonies followed the inquisitional model of summary justice that had emerged in England during the sixteenth century. Crime received notice first in the town courts, an institution administered by the magistrates, a group of saints or redeemed men who pledged, in the words of New Haven's code, to "further the execution of justice according to the righteous rules of God's word."[16] Criminal procedure was left to the discretion of the magistrates, although over time a general pattern emerged. The process usually began when a magistrate learned of a crime and sent the sheriff to bring in the suspect for examination. Less frequently a victim's complaint led to an inquiry. Examinations were private and conducted by the chief magistrate who, with other magistrates in attendance, called upon the defendant to answer the charge. Brought face to face with his accusers, the suspect could contest any allegation, but the examination was not an adversarial proceeding. The magistrates were firmly in control, and their purpose was to gain a confession or to determine the accuracy and sufficiency of the evidence against the accused. Depending on the seriousness of the charge, they could punish the offender summarily, commit him to a public trial, or, for capital cases except in New Haven colony, convene a grand jury for formal indictment.[17]

Trial followed speedily upon commitment or indictment, normally occurring within a month at the next court session but sometimes held at special sittings. Magistrates could place capital defendants or repeat offenders in custody, but bail was a positive right available to most suspects. Here the colonial simplification of law made a big advance over English practices, which required page after page in justices' manuals merely to explain when bail could be granted. Even with a more liberal right to bail, suspects usually received only a warning to appear in court. Witnesses were under similar obligation. Few people violated this trust. In New Haven colony, for example, only four defendants out of 201 failed to show after being warned to attend, and no case was ever postponed because of the absence of a witness. The system worked evidently because strong ties of family and association bound offenders to their communities.

Once begun, trials reached conclusion without delay. Continuances were rare; most cases came to verdict within a month or two after the matter reached court. The trial itself was a model of simplicity. Participants included the judge or judges, defendant, witnesses, and jury. Although there was a limited right to counsel, lawyers took no part in the proceedings; the accused faced the court alone. First the presiding magistrate read the allegation and occasionally the testimony gathered at the preliminary examination. Then he called on the defendant to respond. If the accused confessed, sentencing followed; if not, witnesses appeared to verify the charge. Defendants could challenge these witnesses or call their own in rebuttal, but there was no cross-examination of witnesses nor was testimony taken under oath. Everyone responded to the judge, who assumed an active but generally neutral role in the trial. He asked questions and reminded witnesses of their need to testify truthfully. At times, he acted to protect the defendant's rights, ensuring, for example, that a plea was not coerced or that an oath was not used to compel incriminating testimony.[18]

Upon confession or a verdict, the judge passed sentence but not before conferring with deputy magistrates on appropriate punishment for serious crimes. The defendant's attitude was important to the trial's conclusion. Puritans had moved away from retribution as a central aim of criminal justice, believing instead that punishment should serve to restore a fallen conscience. Offenders who acknowledged their guilt and repented found their sentences softened, but recalcitrant criminals received no shelter from the laws' severe penalties.

Several things are worthy of note about trial procedures and the rights of defendants in colonial New England. The scant time required to process a case, the absence of counsel, the avoidance of oaths, the participant judge—all offer striking contrasts to contemporary criminal justice. Perhaps most surprising is the diminished role of the jury. Although secured in written codes and venerated by the common lawyers, seventeenth-century Puritan courts rarely employed juries in criminal trials. In the first decades of settlement the Massachusetts General Court, the colony's representative assembly of freemen, stood on equal footing with the jury as a means for trying capital cases. New Haven's code abolished juries, placing all cases, even felonies, before the magistrates. For three separate five-year periods, Plymouth colony had not a single criminal jury trial. One study discovered only four jury trials for non-capital cases in the Bay Colony before 1660.[19] What explains this seeming disregard for one of the rights that migration Englishmen claimed to prize so dearly?

Doubtless one reason was the scattered and thinly settled population, a condition that made empanelling a jury troublesome, time consuming, and expensive. Compared to England, even the better established New England counties were sparsely inhabited. As late as 1700, the whole population of Massachusetts barely equalled that of the average English county. Yet more was at issue than mere inconvenience because this circumstance did not prevent the increasing use of civil juries. Of greater moment was the nature of government in the Puritan colonies. Powerful magistrates dominated these colonies. Even though they expressed strong concern for individuals, or at least for the condition of their souls, their primary allegiance was to God and their central goal was to create a righteous settlement. They held a sacred trust to discover and punish sin and, in the process, to reclaim the sinner. To this end, the orthodox colonies adopted a criminal justice system that was more inquisitorial than adversarial. Magistrates ferreted out crime, compiled evidence, questioned witnesses and accused, passed judgment, and imposed sentence. Their responsibilities were too awesome to trust to a jury. Through a combination of severe inquiry and compassion for the truly repentant, magistrates could best maintain the purity of the colony.

In a theme that explains much of American legal history, local conditions and expectations had defined the terms of justice. The New England colonies were created for religious ends. To fit them for their task of reform, unity was necessary. Sin produced disunity; it introduced selfishness into the body politic. A failure to punish known sin would break the saints' covenant with God. The most godly and experienced men, the magistrates, held the responsibility for keeping the colony true to its sacred pledge. When faced with wrongdoing, their task was to secure confession and repentance, not denial of guilt. An adversarial legal system, with its central role for an unguided jury, was unnecessary, inefficient, and, to some extent, dangerous. Summary justice was better suited to the end of maintaining unity. Even defendants had little to gain from jury trials, at least in the absence of other elements of an adversarial process. Placing oneself on the country, the ancient phrase for jury trial, signaled a lack of contrition, a precarious state for the accused if found guilty. And since magistrates showed themselves lenient when they discerned true repentance, where was the advantage in seeking the judgment of one's peers?

A summary procedure may have suited the leaders of New England, but it did not satisfy settlers who increasingly came to the colonies for reasons other than religious fervor. Finding themselves outside the Puritan orbit, new arrivals began to demand jury trial as a shield against governments that viewed them with suspicion. The first evidence of change came with the Massachusetts Body of Liberties (1641), a document reluctantly agreed to in part because the colonial charter required conformity to the laws of England and, by extension, the rights of Englishmen, including the right to trial by jury. The magistracy opposed judgment by peers not because it was less mindful of due process— Puritan opposition to forced self-incrimination, for example, stood in stark contrast to the prevailing practice in English courts of the day—but because it placed power in the hands of the lesser saints. Yet time and circumstances were against the magistrates. Once the Puritan colonies came under royal control, non-saints could sit on juries, and, not surprisingly, more defendants demanded jury trial. By the eighteenth century, with the colony no longer responsible to God for the sin in its midst, this right of the accused more closely fit the model proposed in the Body of Liberties some sixty years earlier.

To the south, in the Chesapeake colonies, migrating Englishmen were also wrestling with the meaning of due process. Virginians did not bring with them the reforming zeal displayed by the Puritans. Living in a royal colony, they had good reason to avoid drastic changes in what they understood to be required by common law. Even so, experimentation was a hallmark of justice in the Old Dominion, just as it had been in

Massachusetts. Again, part of the explanation lies in the small and thinly distributed population. It proved virtually impossible to duplicate the system of English courts, assuming that this was the aim, which it was not. Sour experiences with the complex legal system of the mother country led Virginians to adopt a two-tiered court structure that was simpler than most colonies.[20] Simplification was also a theme in the area of procedure, although not necessarily by design. The colony's justices were innocent of formal training in law, yet the Virginia legislature did not draft any rules for conducting trials in an orderly manner. Left to their own devices, judges called upon personal experience or knowledge gained from standard English texts to help them fashion an understandable and functional criminal process.

Virginians discovered that much of English practice was transferable to the new world. By the 1620s, the colonists had settled on the steps required for a fair criminal procedure: indictment, arrest, bail, examination, trial, judgment, and execution of sentence. But the meaning of these forms was subject to change, even if the outline paralleled traditional process. Sometimes the changes were minor, such as the issuance of an oral summons rather than a written arrest warrant to compel attendance at court. In other instances, alterations were more substantive. Because it was difficult in a sparsely settled country to secure a full panel of potential jurors, Virginia judges turned to the use of bystanders at court to constitute the promised jury of peers, even though jurors were often not from the same neighborhood.[21]

Virginia employed two methods of trying criminal defendants—summarily by justices of the peace or by a jury, neither of which offered widespread protection to the accused. Summary judgment was the preferred procedure, not only for petty crimes, as was commonplace in England, but frequently for felonies also. It was swift and efficient justice and provided for certain punishment. All prosecutions began with an indictment, according to well-established common law procedures. But unlike Massachusetts, which counseled innocence until proven guilty, indictment in Virginia carried a presumption of guilt. As a result, most defendants appeared before a judge and pled guilty rather than bear court costs attendant upon a full trial. The process was not as unfair to defendants as it may seem. It was difficult to conceal crime in such a small society. There was little privacy, and for most offenses witnesses or victims were readily available. Undoubtedly, this is why Virginians considered indictment tantamount to conviction. If everyone knew who committed the offense, then why go to the expense of a trial?

Also, jury trial offered no better protection for defendants. There was no right to counsel, the accused did not know the evidence against him, and he could not call witnesses on his behalf. There was little time, moreover, to prepare a defense. The judicial process was swift, especially for misdemeanors or petty offenses. A grand jury indicted upon evidence gained by justices during the preliminary examination; the judge asked the defendant for a plea, and if "not guilty," empanelled a trial jury; witnesses were heard; and the jurors delivered a verdict. These steps usually occurred in one day, often in a morning or afternoon.

Capital crimes took somewhat longer, if only because the General Court in Williamsburg had sole jurisdiction over felonies. In such cases, an entourage of witnesses, and sometimes jurors, proceeded from the county to the colonial capitol where more experienced judges would hear the case. But the accused received no benefit from the higher tribunal. Judges were at greater remove from the local community and had little concern for mitigating circumstances. Their primary interest was the preservation of order. Procedural regularity was less desirable than prompt action. So trials moved swiftly, with execution of judgment following hard upon the passing of sentence. As was true with lesser crimes, there was no appeal from the court's decision.

Even the limited procedural guarantees available to the colony's free citizens were not available to its servants and slaves. For these classes, summary justice prevailed almost to the exclusion of jury trials. White servants at least had the option of requesting a jury, although most declined because even if they could prove innocence they could not bear the expense of jurors' fees. Slaves did not have this option. Local magistrates tried their cases quickly and without evident concern for procedural regularity.[22]

There is some irony in the failure of Virginians to afford better protection to the accused while they simultaneously protested the Stuart Kings' attempts to forego traditional English rights. But this conclusion is available only from a modern perspective. Virginians transplanted English institutions faithfully, albeit in abbreviated form, and they mirrored English attitudes toward crime and punishment. As in Massachusetts, crime was the reflection of sin in society but, unlike the Puritans, the Chesapeake colonists did not believe in the possibilities of redemption. They shared the same assumptions as the mother country: sin was a threat to social order; it required swift and certain punishment; the graver the sin, the greater the punishment. Massachusetts and its sister colonies could better afford a certain leniency in their legal system. There, colonists shared similar backgrounds and the church and town provided alternate means of social control. Virginia did not have this luxury. Its widespread population, composed primarily of poor males, servants, and an increasing number of African slaves, strained the weak social fabric. Individual rights gave way to the need for order; a retributive criminal law appeared to offer the best protection for property and lives.

In both New England and the Chesapeake colonies—indeed, in all the colonies—certain themes serve to define the rights enjoyed by criminal defendants. Law followed an English model. The new world environment allowed and to some extent encouraged reform, but colonists used this freedom to modify common law, not abandon it. They trimmed the intricate and technical forms of criminal law and adopted simplified procedures that were expressed in plain language. Legislators extracted from the great mass of English precedent the safeguards they considered essential to a fair criminal process and placed these in written codes, with one such code, the Massachusetts Body of Liberties, serving as a model for later bills of rights. In so doing they marked a clear advance over common law practice and made the whole notion of rights more durable than when left to memory and practice alone. The fact that rights at trial did not always correspond to rights in theory should not startle observers of contemporary American justice, nor should it diminish the scope of colonial accomplishments.

The written expression of these rights may have reflected long-held desires of English reformers, but it took the unique seventeenth-century combination of political instability, social upheaval, and economic uncertainties along with the expansive possibilities of a new world to bring them into being. As the colonies matured there was an increasing emphasis on form and order that blunted the further elaboration of rights. In numerous ways an ''anglicanization'' of colonial political and social structure mimicked what was happening in the mother country. The colonies were no longer young. They had larger, more diverse populations that were rapidly gaining a reputation for unruliness, at least by old world standards. Also, they no longer stood so completely outside the control of the mother country. Membership in the empire exerted pressures for uniformity that reinforced the more conservative English practice of law and government. Certainly the eighteenth-century diminution of reform and leniency as principles of colonial justice, marked by a growing tendency to exact the full measure of law in capital cases, paralleled the increased rigor of criminal penalties in England.

The final decades of colonial America also witnessed the emergence of a professional bar, with numerous lawyers crossing the Atlantic to receive instruction at the Inns of Court, the venerable London legal academies. Now, the arcane language and forms of the law became valuable instruments to promote the interests of an elite group.[23] The results were mixed. Once it became the province of the lawyers, criminal procedure grew more remote and complex, but it also placed additional barriers between the state and accused. Perhaps more important, the rise of lawyers created a class of men versed in the forms of law and capable of drawing upon its traditions and articulating its purposes in a setting more conducive to reform. That opportunity would come with the American Revolution.

When discussing rights of the accused, it is tempting to draw a direct line of descent from the colonial period to contemporary America. The language of rights is similar, but not its substance. Due process of law held a sharply different meaning for the seventeenth and eighteenth centuries than it does for the twentieth. Procedural fairness was important; without this concern there could not have been even the expression of rights that occurred in colonial documents. But the good order of society took precedence over the liberty of the individual. In this sense, colonial men were closer to medieval ways of thinking than to modern ones. The language of individualism was only in the process of creation during the decades of settlement. It is anachronistic and misleading to place this theme too prominently in the colonial mind.

What then was the colonial contribution to the development of due process for the accused? It was not so much the creation of a list of rights but more the adoption of a set of attitudes. A penchant for experimentation and reform, a desire to simplify the law and make it accessible in written form to every citizen, a reverence for the traditions of the English past—all these attitudes became hallmarks of an American concern for individual liberties. The colonists' greatest contribution, however, was an acceptance of legal change and a willingness to mold law to social needs and circumstances. Due process, in the words of Felix Frankfurter, "gathered meaning from experience."[24] Flexibility in form and function became a trait that not only defined an American society, it also allowed the ancient maxim of due process to become as expansive as the continent itself.

2

THE REVOLUTIONARY LEGACY

In 1831 Harvard president Josiah Quincy told the young French traveller Alexis de Tocqueville that the only consequence of the American Revolution was to "put the people's name in place of that of the King. For the rest one finds that nothing changed among us."[1] It is one of the paradoxes of the Revolution that such an assertion cannot be dismissed easily. Certainly from the lofty perch of a self-satisfied Boston Brahmin it must have seemed that the world remained largely what it always had been. Americans were no longer part of the British Empire, but otherwise the revolution produced no large-scale social or political upheaval, at least when compared to the bloodier and more radical events in France just thirteen years after 1776. Life for Quincy and thousands of his fellow citizens was scarcely different from the later colonial period, although demographic and economic expansion inevitably quickened its rhythms.

Yet the American world had changed. Emerging from the Revolution was a new ideological order, one that employed an older vocabulary to advance a markedly different conception of reality. The political philosophy that embraced and supported centralized power exercised by the King-in-Parliament gave way in the thirteen rebellious colonies to a new constitutional scheme of divided power and federalism. An optimistic appraisal of man's rational nature and his ability to control his baser instincts began to supplant traditional views of man's capacity for evil, an attribute that required the strong controlling hand of government. Much of this change was hidden by a conservative rhetoric that called for the restoration of ancient liberties. Such language should not obscure the extent of change: a desire to return to a mythical golden age that the present threatens to destroy is a hallmark of revolutionary minds.[2]

Central to the new order was an old idea, the importance of rights to liberty. Indeed, the protection of rights became the focal point of the crusade against the mother country. Scholars have long debated the issue, but it is difficult to imagine a separation without the colonists' conviction that their rights as Englishmen were in grave danger of extinction. The theme of protest was too constant, the tone of argument too insistent, to doubt the primacy of this issue to the revolutionary cause.

Americans, like their British cousins, believed that they had a birthright in the English constitution; the rights they enjoyed were a matter of personal inheritance. These rights were customary and immemorial. They had existed since a dim and ancient past or, in the quaint phrase from English commentaries, since a time "to which the memory of man runneth not." Rights were also immutable. They existed because they were fundamental to the very conception of liberty itself, not because a legislative body established them as positive law.[3]

Colonists entered the struggle for independence with a seventeenth-century view that rights restrained the exercise of power, especially that of government; they did not free the individual from community norms or change the local character of justice. Rights were necessary to secure property and promote a responsible liberty, which in the political lexicon of the day meant to be free of arbitrary power from whatever source. The emphasis was always on the need to limit power, which to good Englishmen everywhere was the chief enemy of liberty. Rights were also the community's protection against unwarranted interference in its affairs by agents of a distant, central authority. A belief that rights liberated individuals, not the community, was the product of a later age.[4]

Changes in eighteenth-century English political theory challenged the colonial view of inalienable, community-based rights. The triumph of Parliament in the century-old struggle for supremacy led to the view that the constitution was malleable and that rights existed at the pleasure of the legislature. This argument became increasingly common at mid-century as the ministry at Whitehall abandoned the policy of salutary neglect toward the colonies and attempted to create an empire more responsive to central direction. Although never as extreme as revolutionary rhetoric imagined, the new policies engendered fears that the demands of power would soon require the sacrifice of English rights in America. There could be no liberty without fixed and certain guards against arbitrary action.[5]

Three rights were central to the colonial understanding of liberty: trial by jury, due process of law, and representative government. Jury trial was especially important. Without it all other rights would ultimately fail. Only a jury from the vicinage or neighborhood, unfettered in its judgments, formed an impregnable shield against arbitrary government. The general verdict, that is, a simple reply of guilt or innocence to an accusation of wrongdoing, was the people's most effective weapon against tyranny. The presence of jurors precluded secret trials, secured the citizenry from venal judges, purchased testimony, or threatening officials, and protected them from other abuses by governments unconcerned with the liberties of its people. It was, quite simply, the best method available of assuring justice and protecting liberty.[6]

Colonial constitutional thought generally mirrored British ideals, but in the case of the jury Americans viewed this ancient right in ways that made them more sensitive to changes in its form or function. One difference was an emerging conception of the jury as a democratic instrument. In Great Britain the jury of peers meant that men without rank or title—in other words, "commoners"—sat in judgment of other commoners. The son of a duke could serve on a jury for the trial of a day-laborer because both were part of that great mass of common people; they were, in that sense, equals. But the English belief in class did not permit the laborer to sit in judgment of his social superior. Americans placed a different twist on the meaning of peers, one more suited to their experiences in a society with fewer and more fluid class boundaries. Here, lawyers such as John Adams began to suggest, peers meant members of the same social and economic class, so that jury trial served as a lower-class check on arbitrary governmental action. This idea was muted in the 1770s, really only a descant on a traditional theme, but it would grow quickly in the more favorable democratic climate of later decades.

Localism was a more important American attachment to the meaning of jury trial. The notion was not new to English law. Since the thirteenth century most trials had been held in the area where the dispute arose or crime occurred. Colonial isolation from England and the new world's pattern of scattered settlements inevitably strengthened the conviction that justice rested on community norms. Evidence from Massachusetts reveals why colonists were so insistent on this view. The Bay Colony freely received the common law of England as the basis of its legal system and with it the doctrine that precedent provided a sure guide to the law. But local communities also reserved the right for juries to determine both the law and facts of any case. This expansive conception of the jury's role restrained judicial authority by removing from the judge the right to decide which precedent applied to the issue at hand. Simultaneously, it permitted local juries to reject by means of an acquittal whatever parts of the law were inconsistent with the community's views of justice and morality. Parliamentary innovations of the 1760s and 1770s challenged this role for the local jury and made revolutionaries place an even higher value on its preservation.[7]

The first assault on the right to trial by jury came with the Stamp Act in 1765. Refusal to pay the stamp tax or to use taxed paper as required by the new law resulted in prosecution before the vice admiralty court, a civil-law tribunal established seventy-five years earlier to enforce imperial trade regulations. Next to taxation without representation, Boston voters proclaimed, "the Jurisdiction of the Admiralty, are our greatest grievance." What troubled the colonists was that vice-admiralty courts operated without juries. In these courts a judge appointed by the crown determined all issues of law and fact: local custom no longer defined the bounds of justice; local communities forfeited much of their ability to blunt parliamentary encroachments on the rights of Englishmen; and local citizens lost the prized assurance of fair trial under common law. "[W]e are obliged," the people of Newburyport complained, "to submit to a Jurisdiction . . . where the Laws of Justinian are the Measure of Right, and the Common Law, the collected wisdom of the British Nation for Ages, is not admitted." Civil law, all Englishmen knew, was the tool of arbitrary governments; common law, the protector of liberty. The threat was obvious and grave.[8]

Faced with protests from the unified colonies, Parliament repealed the Stamp Act. There had been good reason to seek other tribunals for the enforcement of imperial law—local juries were notoriously lax to convict—but in so doing the central government had trampled on one of the most fundamental and sensitive English rights and seriously eroded the colonists' faith in the security of their liberties. Unfortunately, the various ministries did not heed for long the arguments concerning the inviolability of the right to trial by jury. Nine years later, after a series of measures that brought impassioned defense of other rights, Parliament passed the Massachusetts Administration of Justice Act, one of the so-called Intolerable Acts adopted in response to the Boston Tea Party and continued infringements of imperial regulations. This law allowed royal officials to seek a change of venue or location for prosecutions under the navigation acts. There was no denial of trial by jury, only of trial by jury from the neighborhood. The act was clearly designed to aid prosecution by shifting the trial to a site less hostile to the needs of empire. The colonial response was the same: "the respective colonies," the Declaration and Resolves of the First Continental Congress solemnly intoned, "are entitled to the the common law of England, and more especially to the great and inestimable privilege of being tried by their peers of the vicinage, according to the course of that law."[9]

Even though trial by jury was a bedrock principle of English liberty, the colonists did not defend it to the exclusion of other rights that they believed to be in jeopardy. By 1776 they had developed a litany of grievances by which they expressed their conviction that the government in London had abandoned the English constitution in a vain quest for imperial power. Rebel leaders did not manufacture these complaints to justify separation for more mundane reasons. Grievances, after all, are the other side of rights. An expression of a grievance in the eighteenth century was an allegation of a right violated. The series of charges made by Americans constituted a schedule of those rights they considered vital to liberty.[10] Significantly, but not unexpectedly given the structure of authority within the empire, rights of the accused were prominent on the list.

One of the earliest colonial grievances concerned general warrants, called writs of assistance, which customs officials used to search colonial property for contraband or smuggled goods. As with many of the complaints against the mother country, this issue already had a long history when resistance surfaced in 1761 to the unlimited power of search and seizure granted under cover of the writs.[11]

The Tudors had introduced a broad search and seizure power to England during the reign of Henry VIII. Invoked most frequently to suppress seditious printing, this royal prerogative met only scattered and ineffectual resistance until the Glorious Revolution of 1688. Among those to suffer was Sir Edward Coke, who lay on his deathbed as emissaries from the Privy Council ransacked his study and library, taking away notes and manuscripts, including the folios for all four parts of his masterwork, the *Institutes*. Limits first appeared on the power during the reign of William and Mary, when Parliament repealed a tax law because the searches required for its enforcement were "a badge of slavery upon the whole people, exposing every man's house to be entered into, and searched by persons unknown to him." This sentiment found repeated expression in parliamentary debates during succeeding decades as the power came under attack.[12]

Also arrayed against general search warrants was the force of common law. Coke had argued that the common law gave no power, general or specific, "to break open any man's house to search for a felon or stolen goods either in the day or night."[13] Other commentators took a more moderate approach. Sir Matthew Hale, in his influential *History of the Pleas of the Crown,* reflected the emerging legal opinion. Like Coke, he rejected the general warrant because it allowed officers to conduct unbridled searches without having to justify their actions. But he also concluded that judges could issue specific warrants upon a request that demonstrated probable cause and that described with particularity the goods or persons sought and the places to be searched.[14] One thing was certain to all commentators: the decision to issue a warrant was a judicial, not an executive, act.

Opposition to general search warrants mounted throughout the eighteenth century. Two cases in the 1760s brought the issue into sharp focus. In 1762 John Wilkes, a radical Whig member of Parliament, attacked the goverment in the *North Briton,* a series of pamphlets in which one issue, Number 45, proved especially odious. Lord Halifax, the Secretary of State, issued a general warrant to four messengers ordering the arrest of those involved and the seizure of their papers. Wilkes and his printers brought suit against the messengers for false imprisonment and received damages after Chief Justice Pratt told the jury that "to enter a man's house by virtue of a nameless warrant in order to procure evidence, is worse than the Spanish Inquisition; a law under which no Englishman would wish to live for an hour."[15]

Three years later a similar incident resulted in a defeat for the government's action in the case of *Entick* v. *Carrington.* Pratt, now elevated to the peerage as Lord Camden, upheld the verdict on appeal, declaring that the government's action, if permitted, would open "the secret cabinets and bureaus of every subject in this kingdom

. . . whenever the secretary of state shall think fit to charge, or even suspect, a person . . . of seditious libel." By the eve of the American Revolution the Earl of Chatham, Sir William Pitt, could give eloquent voice to what had become the opinion of Englishmen: "The poorest man may in his cottage bid defiance to all the force of the Crown. It may be frail—its roof may shake—the wind may blow through it—the storm may enter—the rain may enter—but the King of England cannot enter; all his forces dare not cross the threshold of that ruined tenement."[16]

General warrants declined rapidly as a tool against seditious libel, but the power to issue writs of assistance, previously authorized by Parliament as part of the customs laws, remained unimpaired. Britons did not object much to broad search and seizure powers in this area, perhaps because the writs were used infrequently in the search for smuggled goods in England. The American experience was dramatically different. Not surprisingly, the matter came to a head in Boston, one of the busiest colonial ports and the center of much underground trade.

In Massachusetts, as elsewhere, customs officials at one time could enter and search buildings simply on the authority of their royal commissions. Opposition to this practice resulted first in warrants issued by the governor, then in 1755 by the Superior Court, the highest court in the colony. These writs carried broad powers and were perpetual for the life of the king. No one tested the warrants' legality, however, until 1761 when sixty-three Boston merchants retained James Otis, Jr., to challenge the issuance of new writs since the old ones expired the previous year upon the death of George II. Otis's presentation is justly remembered because it asserted the supremacy of fundamental law over legislative power. The particulars of his claim were equally memorable. As a young lawyer, John Adams witnessed the trial and later recalled the argument: the writs, Otis declared, went "against the fundamental principles of law, the privilege of house. . . . [It was] the worst instrument of arbitrary power, the most destructive of English liberty, that was ever found in an English law-book."[17]

Otis lost the case, but not his cause. After the passage of the Stamp Act Boston mobs thwarted efforts of officials to search and seize suspicious goods. Elsewhere provincial courts refused to grant the writ. Two claims justified their opposition: the common-law requirement of equal treatment forbade the application of a policy in the colonies that was not permitted in England; and the writs were subject to local law, which recognized only specific warrants.[18] The controversy continued until the outbreak of war, even though writs of assistance were of no practical effect after the mid-1760s. As the period of constitution-making would demonstrate, Americans had found in this issue one of the fundamental rights of the accused that was essential to liberty. Significantly, it was a right not previously included in colonial charters, enactments, or declarations.[19]

Other grievances pointed to additional rights. "An Address to the Inhabitants of Quebec," drafted in 1774 by the First Continental Congress to encourage Canadian resistance to the continued use of civil law in their provinces, listed the writ of habeas corpus as another invaluable right of Englishmen. No one in Britain or America disputed the fundamental nature of this safeguard. What worried the colonists was the apparent ease with which Parliament dismissed its application to one part of the empire. They feared the precedent it might set.

The same letter to Quebec contained a much fuller description of the rights of trial by jury than had previously appeared in colonial protests. The jury should be composed of twelve men from the same neighborhood who could reasonably know the reputation of the defendant and the witnesses and whose verdict would be fair because a false judgment formed a precedent that "may militate against themselves." Further, the trial should be held in open court and a full enquiry conducted "face to face." The tone of the letter and the care it took in describing the necessary conditions of basic English rights suggest that delegates anticipated the day when these guarantees would need to be incorporated into a new political canon.[20]

In 1776 the litany of rights denied reached its fullest expression in the Declaration of Independence. Numerous British actions, the document charged, robbed colonial Englishmen of their birthright. Dependent judges who served at the King's pleasure, feigned trials for British soldiers accused of murder, trans-Atlantic changes of venue for violations of trade laws, deprivation of trial by jury—each item mocked an essential ingredient of English liberty, namely, the guarantee of justice fairly administered according to the due process of law.

Much of the revolutionary rhetoric now seems exaggerated. Few Englishmen in America suffered any actual loss of their rights because of the enforcement of parliamentary statutes. British officials in the colonies rarely sought to remove trials from the community, even though they well understood that local juries often made prosecution a futile exercise. Colonists quickly blunted the force of general warrants. But what actually occurred is not the complete measure of truth for revolutionaries. Threat is an equally strong reason for resistance. To many Americans of the 1770s the challenge to their traditional liberties was real and pervasive.

The grievances that stirred such passions before 1776 reflected a more limited set of rights than the list embodied in revolutionary state constitutions and later in the federal Bill of Rights. In the process of creating new governments, Americans began to identify those rights important to their conception of ordered liberty. This search was wide-ranging. The articulation of rights was not confined simply to those issues that had arisen in the struggle with Great Britain. The rebels understood that their separation was the first step in the creation of a new political society. No longer strangers in the promised land, they would seize the opportunity that history provided to participate in a great experiment to expand the meaning of liberty. Their recent experiences also persuaded them that these fundamental rights deserved formal protection in written constitutions.

Virginia, the oldest colony, led the movement toward a new constitutional order. On May 15, 1776, the Virginia Convention, an extralegal body that bridged the gap between royal control and independence, adopted two resolutions, one instructing the Virginia delegates at the Continental Congress to seek separation from Great Britain and the second calling for a committee to draft a statement of rights. Less than two weeks later the committee of twenty-eight men reported the results of their work, and the Convention approved a Declaration of Rights on June 12. The ease with which the document was drafted and its authorship by George Mason, an unschooled planter who lacked access to the classic defenses of English liberty, reveal how powerful a consensus had developed among Americans on the nature and extent of their fundamental rights.

Much of the Declaration addressed procedural guarantees available to the criminally accused. Many of the safeguards were familiar to readers conversant with English antecedents and colonial charters and statutes. Repeated from prior documents was an injunction against cruel and unusual punishments taken verbatim from the English Bill of Rights of

1688, a pledge of due process using language reminiscent of the Magna Carta, and the ancient right of trial by jury of the vicinage. But Mason was not content merely to compile rights enumerated elsewhere. The colonial experience had taught the value of spelling out carefully and completely the penumbras of liberty. The privilege against general warrants received particular mention. So too did the protection against self-incrimination. The right to a jury trial also took on additional coloration: the trial must be speedy; the defendant had to be confronted with his accusers and witnesses; he could call for evidence in his favor; and the jury's verdict must be unanimous. Here were the requirements of procedural justice that the Fourth, Fifth, Sixth, and Eighth Amendments would later incorporate.[21]

Virginia was not alone in the desire to place guarantees beyond the reach of government. The movement toward written constitutions that expressed fundamental law was commonplace in the revolutionary states. Nine of the new constitutions contained separate bills of rights that served as preambles, while the other four incorporated protection of specific rights into the frame of government. Some of these documents provided safeguards not mentioned in the Virginia Declaration. Other states extended the right of counsel to all criminal defendants, with "the same privileges," in the language of New Jersey's constitution, "as their prosecutors are or shall be entitled to." In addition to counsel, Pennsylvania's document further decorated the criminal process by requiring that all prosecutions be undertaken in the name of the state, that the legislature protect against "every corruption or partiality in the choice, return, or appointment of juries," that punishments be made less sanguinary and proportionate to the crime, and that prisons be established where offenders could work at hard labor. Maryland included an express prohibition against bills of attainder, a legislative act usually aimed at persons suspected of treason, which pronounced guilt without benefit of judicial process. The state also required an indictment before prosecution could begin. Georgia stipulated that "no grand jury shall consist of less than eighteen, and twelve may find a bill [of indictment]."[22]

Clearly, something was happening to expand previous conceptions of rights of the accused. Revolutionaries began to endorse guarantees that until 1776 had received scant notice or that went well beyond the precedents of common law. The right to counsel is a striking example of how far the founders were willing to advance indivdual rights. Both in

Great Britain and the colonies a person charged with a felony had no right at common law to the advice or representation of counsel. For less serious crimes, misdemeanors, counsel was permitted. Not until 1836 did Parliament extend the right to counsel to all criminal defendants. Since felonies almost always were capital offenses, the common law fostered an irony wherein persons facing fines or light punishments could claim the assistance of counsel, but not those defendants whose loss at trial could lead to the gallows. Few people protested this apparent lack of balance. Judges were supposed to be the neutral protectors of an accused's rights, and the potential threat to order was too great to allow the obfuscations of lawyers to delay or deny justice.[23]

Experience was a great teacher, but more was at work than continued reliance on past grievances to define rights. In part, the newness of their enterprise demanded that framers take great care in specifying rights, and their inquiry into what was necessary for the protection of liberty inevitably took them beyond the realm of history. What rights were necessary to effect happiness and advance the great experiment in liberty? Were civil rights and natural rights the same? Could rights be added onto or subtracted from? Even if one accepted Thomas Paine's commonsense formulation that bills of rights should be ''a plain positive declaration of the rights themselves'' and that they represented ''a sort of common stock, which, by the consent of all, may be occasionally used for the benefit of any,'' there was still need to identify what rights could receive such endorsement.[24]

Ideas from three sources other than direct experience—British legal commentary, revolutionary republicanism, and Enlightenment philosophy—influenced the identification of procedural safeguards for the accused. Legal writings appealed to Americans, who valued the common law as their heritage. Coke's authority was widely acknowledged, but in the 1770s lawmakers and jurists more often subscribed to Sir William Blackstone's newly penned *Commentaries* (1765–69). These volumes carried none of the majestic sweep that so marked Coke's writings, but they did explain for Americans the common law as it existed in England immediately prior to separation. Blackstone did not inspire new rights as much as confirm old ones; his work allowed Americans to tie the revolutionary cause more closely to the protection of long-standing English liberties. Equally important was his description of what those rights meant in the courtroom. This summary had an immediate impact on the development of American law. The colonies had produced no legal literature worthy of note nor were case reports widely available, so Blackstone provided an invaluable guide to practice, especially on points of criminal procedure. The various declarations of rights had employed general language to identify procedural safeguards; the *Commentaries* defined specifically what these guarantees meant. Lawmakers relied on them in the creation of new criminal codes, and jurists found them to be useful guides to the reception of English law into American jurisprudence.[25]

Revolutionary republicanism provided a symbolic context for the identification of rights. Republicanism was not so much a coherent philosophy as it was a series of warnings about the abuse of power, with examples drawn from both ancient and recent history. Liberty inhered in the people and only a morally responsible citizenry could protect it. Republics were best suited to the preservation of liberty because they rested firmly on popular sovereignty. Yet these states were fragile. Their reliance on the civic virtue of the people had in the past proven inadequate to resist the encroachments of power. While the new world offered certain protections against the age-old enemies of liberty—no hereditary aristocracy, no established church, no standing armies: nothing, in other words, that typically buttressed tyrannical regimes—revolutionary republicanism argued that governmental power must be limited in form and function. Only written constitutions with clearly identified restrictions on power provided sufficient protection. Even then the people had to remain vigilant. Power was too seductive to trust any government too much.[26]

If republicanism heightened fears of power, an Enlightenment attitude encouraged an optimistic belief that people were rational and would respond positively to humane and intelligent government. The Enlightenment was a decades-long attack on earlier generations' pessimistic appraisal of man's fundamental nature. Reason, not passion, was at the heart of human psychology. This circumstance lessened the need for strong governments and made monarchy vulnerable to a philosophy that sought the reform of civil society in conformity with a natural world ruled by logical and discoverable laws. Characterized by a disdain for the past, enlightened belief emphasized the possibility of creating a new order. It is no surprise that such a prospect appealed to revolutionaries, even those who sought counsel from history.[27]

Viewed as savage and irrational, criminal justice offered an inviting

target for the crusading energies of Enlightenment thinkers. Most prominent among the reformers were three Frenchmen—Voltaire, Rousseau,
Montesquieu—and an Italian, Cesare Beccaria. Their numerous critiques
condemned the overzealous use of bloody punishments and called for
laws to prevent crimes rather than to seek retribution for wrongdoing.
Man's newfound ability to live by reason had made retributive justice a
vulgar and byzantine concept.[28]

Montesquieu and Beccaria, in particular, found a receptive audience in
America. The Italian's influence was especially notable, primarily because his classic work, *On Crimes and Punishments,* first published in
1764, coincided neatly in time and temperament with the Revolution. In
this manifesto of eighteenth-century liberalism, Beccaria expressed an
ardent faith in the power of reason and the perfectibility of social
institutions. He repeatedly urged that law be used as little as possible to
restrict human freedom. Otherwise, crime increased because men had
more opportunities to violate legal prohibitions. Beccaria offered other
prescriptions for a fair and humane criminal process. Presumption of
innocence should be maintained at every stage of judicial proceedings; all
criminal laws should be fixed and embodied in a written code; in the
public trial by a jury of one's peers, witnesses must be credible, and
evidence certain; punishment had to be strictly limited, proportionate to
the crime, and inflicted with speed and certainty. Once society had
established a rational criminal code, judges could not be allowed too
much discretion to interpret it, nor the executive to set it aside by pardon.
Due process and justice, in sum, demanded checks upon the arbitrary and
capricious authority of government.[29]

Is it any wonder that Americans took Beccaria to heart? Experience
had taught them that he was correct: severe codes did little to diminish
crime. His reformist theories fit the conditions and ideals of the young
republic. The new United States, after all, was not England. America
shared neither a social or economic structure nor a governmental philosophy with her Atlantic cousins. Any difference between the two countries
encouraged a questioning of inherited practices and the adoption of new
ones wherever law violated revolutionary ideals. One result was a
vigorous effort to reform criminal law and penal institutions and to
outline rights that corresponded with man's newly discovered rational
nature.[30]

The effort to identify rights of the accused was surprisingly muted after the first flurry of constitution-making in 1776 and 1777. Various states redrafted these basic documents as revolutionary doctrine more clearly defined who was to create them and what they should contain, but few additional procedural guarantees were added to the growing corpus of rights. Massachusetts was one of the last states to replace its royal charter with a new frame of government. The constitution of 1780 emerged from a convention specially elected for this purpose, after voters, two years earlier, rejected a scheme of government drafted by the existing legislature. More directly than any other constitution of the period, this document reflected the temper of the people-at-large concerning matters of criminal due process.

No new rights of defendants appeared in the declaration of rights that served as preamble to the Massachusetts constitution. The document contained a compendium of acknowledged guarantees that formed the common language of any dialogue concerning the limits on government: trial by jury of the neighborhood, indictment before trial, unanimous verdicts, protection against self-incrimination, right to compulsory process, access to counsel, prosecution only by law of the land, security from unreasonable searches and seizures, protection from excessive bail and cruel or unusual punishments.[31] Thus, by 1780, Americans had identified the rights of the accused that were essential to their collective liberty. The stage was set for the establishment of a federal bill of rights.

Yet the United States Constitution, drafted during a long, hot summer of debate in 1787, contained no such enumeration of rights. Framers generally gave two reasons for the omission, although neither was without dispute. The first concerned the nature of the problem confronting the nation and the theories designed to solve it. The second addressed the question of which government, state or national, had responsibility for protecting the rights of citizens.[32]

Delegates to the Constitutional Convention focused primarily on the authority the new government would require to function effectively. Changes in circumstances and in theory made the creation of a strong central power less troublesome than it had been even a decade earlier. The Articles of Confederation, and its instrument, the Confederation Congress, had not proven equal to the tasks of nationhood. An inability to command unity made the several republics vulnerable to the twin threats of anarchy from within and invasion from without. A new philosophy— or more accurately, new interpretations of republicanism—facilitated the decision to abandon the Confederation and embrace a new political structure. Americans now viewed ultimate power as the sole prerogative of the people. The notion of a sovereign people, a convenient fiction, allowed specified powers to be entrusted to government and permitted these powers to be subdivided among governmental agencies for their more certain control.[33] The creation of a federal system and a formal separation of powers among the legislative, executive, and judicial branches were the devices used to justify the grant of vastly increased authority to the new national government. Under this scheme, the framers contended, government could exercise only those powers delegated to it explicitly in a written constitution. Without express power to legislate—and Congress had no such authority over individual liberties—there could be no threat to the rights of the people.

Another reason for the Constitution's silence was that under the federal system states had the responsibility for protecting civil rights. Civil rights were, by definition, privileges of citizenship. Governments had an obligation to extend rights equally to all citizens and safeguard them against private interference. This obligation was best suited to state governments, which, by their very nature, were closer to the people. The various republican states had already acted appropriately by placing in their constitutions those rights essential to liberty. In several cases, state courts had demonstrated their ability to protect these guarantees against legislative interference, although too often rights were more honored than observed by the people's representatives.

A national constitution, the framers insisted, properly addressed only national matters. "A minute detail of particular rights," Alexander Hamilton argued in *Federalist No. 84,* "is certainly far less applicable to a [United States] constitution . . . , which is merely intended to regulate the general political interests of a nation, than to a constitution which has the regulation of every species of personal and private concerns." The new frame of government did incorporate some key rights as limitations on central power. Article I, Section 9 prohibited Congress from passing bills of attainder or suspending the writ of habeas corpus except for rebellion or invasion, while Article III guaranteed trial by jury in all federal crimes. But, in the main, the framers abided by the tradition that criminal justice, and the rights of the accused, were matters for local concern.

These arguments by defenders of the new constitution (commonly called Federalists) were not persuasive. Debates in the Pennsylvania ratification convention foreshadowed the concerns expressed in other states during 1788. Antifederalists sharply disputed the contention that the Constitution protected rights by limiting to the central government only those powers enumerated in the document. They argued that the new national government so consolidated power that it "must necessarily annihilate and absorb the legislative, executive and judicial powers of the several States, and produce from their ruins . . . an iron handed despotism."[34] Among other things, the Antifederalists feared federal prosecution of state officials for political purposes. But they also recognized how often an all-powerful legislature had claimed authority over the bill of rights in the state constitution. The traditional reliance on the states as guarantors of liberty no longer rested on a firm foundation.

Although there were other deficiencies, Antifederalists judged the Constitution's greatest single omission to be a bill of rights "ascertaining and fundamentally establishing those unalienable and personal rights of men, without the full, free and secure enjoyment of which there can be no liberty, and over which it is not necessary for a good government to have control."[35] As a remedy delegates opposed to the new government submitted a bill of rights to be included in the Constitution before it could become effective. Central to these proposed amendments were the rights of the accused.

The Antifederalists lost in Pennsylvania and elsewhere to the better organized and more persuasive defenders of the Constitution. But their persistent and prescient warnings about the voracious power of government and the fragile nature of liberty commanded such support that, in order to gain ratification, Federalists pledged to submit an amendatory bill of rights before the First Congress. James Madison, congressman from Virginia and the intellectual force behind the Constitution, appeared as the champion of the amendments, even though earlier he thought them merely parchment barriers against a determined legislative majority. Three months after Congress convened, he proposed to the House of Representatives a series of amendments which eventually formed the Bill of Rights. Reaction to his proposals was mixed. Opponents of the measures, convinced that such amendments were unnecessary and perhaps even harmful, engaged the House in a tiresome debate. No one disputed the rights in question; the major controversy concerned whether they achieved any good purpose without changing the nature of the

Constitution. Finally, the House sent seventeen amendments to the Senate, which returned twelve for further consideration. On September 25, 1788, a joint conference reported twelve amendments for approval by the states. Two failed to gain ratification; the remaining ten became the Bill of Rights.[36]

Rights of the accused received major emphasis in the new amendments. Four of the eight substantive articles addressed matters of criminal process so completely that scholars have noted their character as a miniature code of criminal procedure. Twelve specific rights received notice, as did the more general guarantee of due process of law:

ARTICLE IV

The right of the people to be secure in their persons, houses, papers, and effects, against unreasonable searches and seizures, shall not be violated, and no Warrants shall issue, but upon probable cause, supported by Oath or affirmation, and particularly describing the place to be searched, and the persons or things to be seized.

ARTICLE V

No person shall be held to answer for a capital, or otherwise infamous crime, unless on a presentment or indictment of a Grand Jury, except in cases arising in the land or naval forces, or in the Militia, when in actual service in time of War or public danger; nor shall any person be subject for the same offense to be twice put in jeopardy of life or limb; nor shall be compelled in any criminal case to be a witness against himself, nor be deprived of life, liberty, or property, without due process of law; nor shall private property be taken for public use, without just compensation.

ARTICLE VI

In all criminal prosecutions, the accused shall enjoy the right to a speedy and public trial, by an impartial jury of the State and district wherein the crime shall have been committed, which district shall have previously been ascertained by law, and to be informed of the nature and cause of the accusation; to be confronted with the witnesses against him; to have compulsory process for obtaining witnesses in his favor, and to have the Assistance of Counsel for his defence.

ARTICLE VIII

Excessive bail shall not be required, nor excessive fines imposed, nor cruel and unusual punishments inflicted.

The language of the amendments could not have been more recognizable to the American people, who had seen or heard it used repeatedly over one and a half centuries. It was a vocabulary pregnant with meaning but without fixed bounds. What was an unreasonable search? The colonial and revolutionary experience left examples; it did not establish settled definitions. The same was true with double jeopardy, the only right now added that had not been included in the litanies of the period. Here, common law provided an incomplete guide that could not anticipate the federal system's dual power to accuse and try offenders. And what was the meaning of assistance of counsel or excessive bail or cruel and unusual punishments?

These questions would provide a rich source for debate and litigation during the next two hundred years, beginning with state courts and legislatures in the nineteenth century and expanding to federal courts in the twentieth. The founders would likely not have been bothered by the knowledge that these amendments would undergo both challenge and shifts in meaning. They were practical politicians who constructed the Bill of Rights not from abstract political theory but from experience, and they anticipated that future generations would expand the scope of protected rights. Neither did they expect that the Bill of Rights would prevent all injustices. At a minimum, Madison had argued, the written guarantee of rights would serve as "good ground for an appeal to the sense of the community" when threatened by arbitrary governments or oppressive majorities. The various state and federal constitutions would serve as a protective canopy for personal liberty; and the Bill of Rights, in the words of its foremost historian, would send notice to the world that "national independence, without personal liberty, was an empty prize."[37]

3

DUE PROCESS IN
THE NEW REPUBLIC

Leon Radzinowicz, the foremost modern authority on the history of English legal process, has remarked that ''every political revolution brings its own criminal legislation.''[1] The American experience confirms this observation. Stirred by a fear that imperial pretensions threatened their heritage as Englishmen, the revolutionary generation wrote guarantees of rights into its fundamental law. Chief among these safeguards, as the various bills of rights make clear, was a requirement of due process in all criminal proceedings.

Concern for procedural fairness did not disappear with the generation that made the Revolution. To the contrary, it became more intense in the first half of the nineteenth century as the Jacksonian politics of individualism redefined and ultimately replaced republicanism. What remained constant was a desire to restrain governmental power. The interweaving of these two themes—individualism and limited government—explains much of antebellum criminal jurisprudence. Primary emphasis was on the forms of justice, especially the proper method for proceeding against the accused. Technical correctness served as a touchstone of due process. Pre-trial procedures, such as indictment and jury selection, were the subject of much litigation and legislative debate. Conduct of the trial was equally important. State supreme courts, in particular, elaborated more precise standards in matters of confessions and double jeopardy and defined more carefully the relationship of judge and jury.

Developments in criminal process occurred in the midst of and in response to a changing political and social environment. Demographic and territorial expansion was dramatic, even to casual observers. Americans, foreign visitors remarked, were a restless people. A population that barely exceeded three million in 1790 increased tenfold by 1860, while the nation's western boundary shifted 2,000 miles to the Pacific Ocean. Equally striking was the economic transformation spurred by the triumph of capitalism, a philosophy of the marketplace that touted private property, individual initiative, and unrestrained trade as engines of wealth and progress. Rapid advances in transportation facilitated economic growth by opening the interior to settlement and making possible the emergence of cities as regional trade centers. A new form of enterprise, corporations, began to replace traditional partnerships and single-owner businesses, setting the stage for the accumulation of capital and economies of scale that made later industrialization possible. These developments were not unmixed blessings. As markets expanded, the economic power of local communities lessened. And the corporation possessed wealth and power that proved almost as threatening to Americans as the imperial hand of Great Britain had been.

Political changes after the Constitutional Convention were also momentous. The 1790s witnessed vigorous attempts by the Federalists to realize the promise of energetic national government. Their efforts succeeded only in part. The Supreme Court under John Marshall carried the legacy into the 1820s, but Congress and the executive departments, dominated by followers of Thomas Jefferson and, later, Andrew Jackson, defined their role in more limited terms. Government governed best which governed least: this belief, often termed negative government, became a hallmark of the ascendant Democratic party, especially after Jackson's election as president in 1828. One result was that power in the federal system shifted decisively to the states. It was a scheme of federalism that fit the circumstances of the new nation. Even with the advances in transportation and communication, the United States remained more a collection of states than a true nation. Local interests continued to exert a powerful influence, and the exercise of state and local power not only echoed a major theme of republicanism but also tapped a political tradition that had existed since the colonial period.

During this same period, republicanism virtually disappeared as a governing philosophy, supplanted by popular democracy. Again, the election of Jackson symbolized the shift. Republican theory emphasized the restraint of power and defined freedom as the subordination of individual interests to the common good. Democrats also embraced limitations on government, but they identified liberty as the ability to pursue private goals and ambitions, especially economic ones, without undue restraints. The common good came from individuals acting separately to shape their lives and fortunes. Properly constituted, government left people alone and enabled them to pursue their own interests. Economy and efficiency in government, states' rights, and voluntary association were logical corollaries of this new democracy.

These changes, and the ideas that propelled them, had a profound impact on rights of the accused. The legal mirror that reflected these developments came from the states, not from the federal government. Most commentators agreed that the federal Bill of Rights restrained only the Congress, a view confirmed by the Supreme Court's decision in *Barron* v. *Baltimore* (1833), which held that the Fifth Amendment, and by implication the other amendments, did not apply to the states. Earlier, in *United States* v. *Hudson and Goodwin* (1812), the Court had ruled that there was no federal common law of crimes, that is, only Congress could identify crimes under federal law. Since Congress passed relatively few criminal statutes, these two decisions made the due process requirements of the Bill of Rights quite unimportant.[2]

Nineteenth-century criminal law fell primarily within the state's jurisdiction. Rights of the accused found formal expression in state constitutions. During two waves of constitutional reform—first in the 1820s and then in the 1850s—state conventions incorporated most of the federal protections for criminal defendants in their new charters. Even the language was similar. But consensus on a list of rights did not lead to common definitions of those guarantees. Criminal process varied markedly from state to state. To a degree unrecognized today, state legislatures and courts provided the primary impetus for defining and extending the rights of the accused.

Protection of defendants' rights depended in large measure on an independent judiciary. In proposing amendments to the federal Constitution, James Madison predicted that judges "will consider themselves in a peculiar manner the guardian of those rights; . . . they will be naturally led to resist every encroachment upon rights expressly stipulated for in the constitution by the declaration of rights."[3] Madison's prophecy was accurate, but he could not foresee the nineteenth-century shift in the role of judges or the degree of change it would bring to an understanding of due process.

The revolutionary generation envisioned judges as declarers of a fixed and unchanging law that embraced immutable principles of natural justice. Judges could not make law; they simply discovered pre-existing standards from the common law and applied them to individual cases in order to achieve a fair result. Lawmaking authority rested with elected representatives of the people, the legislature alone. Judicial innovation was an impermissible exercise of power.

Changes in the conception of law itself and a corresponding new role for courts began during the first two decades after the Revolution with an attack on the unpredictability and uncertainty of common law. Gaining momentum from the political struggles of the 1790s, the assault highlighted common law's inability to provide a guide for future conduct. Not only did its meaning vary from state to state, but its focus was individual and retrospective, applying a standard of behavior to acts that had already occurred. Such uncertainty vested too much authority in judges, a condition that ultimately threatened liberty. "It subjects the citizen to punishment," proclaimed the Virginia legislature in 1800, "according to the judiciary will, when he is left in ignorance of what this law enjoins as a duty, or prohibits as a crime."[4]

By the 1820s the success of this attack was clear. In his influential *Historical Sketches of the Principles and Maxims of American Jurisprudence,* Ohio lawyer John Milton Goodenow argued that a judge "is *governed* himself by *positive* law, and executes and inforces the will of the supreme power, which is the will of THE PEOPLE." Popular sovereignty had replaced natural justice as the foundation of law. This new idea meant that legislative or statute law was supreme over common law, and the court, in the words of one commentator, "must take the law as it is, and by all due and proper means execute it, without any pretense to judge of its right or wrong."[5] Under this notion, law was an instrument of social policy used to advance liberty.

Most antebellum commentators accepted the view that all law, even common law, was simply an expression of majority will. The shift in the meaning of law could hardly have been more dramatic. Previously, common law acted as a restraint on governmental power. Strict adherence to earlier decisions, no matter how distant in time or space, protected liberty by limiting the power of an arbitrary ruler. This traditional veneration of precedent quickly gave way to a more flexible view that legal rules were valuable only when they allowed men to plan their affairs rationally. Certainty in law was necessary, not to protect society from the tyrant but to free individuals to pursue material gain, the lodestar of true liberty for nineteenth-century Americans. The implications for economic growth were obvious and profound, but the change also affected rights of defendants. Criminal due process, like the rest of law, would not be bound rigidly to precedent. It too would respond to the needs of a free society, with elected judges claiming the responsibility of re-casting the common law in democratic language and forms.

Nowhere was this new attitude more apparent than in the law controlling criminal indictment. Formal accusation by the grand jury, acting as representatives of the community, began the criminal process and was subject to rigorous scrutiny by trial and appellate courts. Judges had always interpreted strictly the technical language used to frame indictments and quashed or voided charges that failed to follow the prescribed form. In doing so, they followed the rule laid down by treatise writers that "it is . . . advisable to attend, with the greatest nicety, to the words . . . ; the broad principle . . . renders strict adherence essential." Courts gave two reasons for such strictness: the prisoner needed proper knowledge of the charge to prepare his defense; and the indictment's precision barred a second trial for the same offense.[6]

Despite the common-law emphasis on correct form, antebellum appellate courts usually hesitated to overturn a conviction when the substance of the charge was clear. "We consider it our duty," concluded the Indiana Supreme Court in 1822, "to give all weight to objections however nice and technical . . . but we would guard against the evil of giving too easy an ear to such as rest on mere form of words, and can have no possible bearing on the merits of the case . . . an evil which has long and justly been complained of as a disease of the law." Judges drew the line at facts material to the charge. An indictment had to state these facts precisely. Thus an accusation of receiving stolen goods did not have to cite when or where the goods were stolen because the defendant was not charged with larceny. But an indictment for passing counterfeit bank notes had to include an exact description of the notes; otherwise, the defendant could not claim the protection of double jeopardy in future prosecutions for the same offense.[7]

By the 1840s and 1850s procedural formalism was on the wane as state legislatures ratified by statute the modifications initiated by the courts. A desire to codify the law, using commonsense formulations and stating them in plain English, provided much of the impetus for change. Also important was a growing concern that an undue proceduralism threatened social order by "facilitating, unnecessarily, the escape of the guilty." The shift was generally away from excessive formality only. Courts continued to hold prosecutors and grand juries to strict standards on the substance of the accusation. Otherwise, the Indiana court noted, "the harmless decision of today becomes the dangerous precedent of tomorrow. The people have no better security than in holding the officers of the state to a reasonable degree of care, precision, and certainty, in prosecuting the citizen for a violation of the law." The regard for procedural requirements in criminal cases was no "idle technicality"; it was a "safe and salutary public policy . . . supported by the weightiest of reasons."[8]

In spite of the pronounced Anglophobia that infected American politics after the Revolution, state courts relied heavily on British precedents to guide their definitions of due process, at least until a body of native legal opinion emerged. The law of confession, a bellwether of society's attitude toward the criminal defendant, is illustrative. In 1783, a landmark English case, *Rex* v. *Warickshall,* held that "a confession forced from the mind by the flattery of hope, or by the torture of fear, comes in so questionable a shape when it is to be considered as evidence of guilt, that no credit ought to be given it."[9] This decision set the standard for most American courts. Judges cited the need for trustworthy evidence and the defendant's privilege against self-incrimination as reasons for adopting the rule. But *Warickshall* excluded only confessions stemming from official violence or promises. Interrogation was an acceptable way to gain confessions, although most treatise writers did not commend the practice, and deception, trickery, or psychological pressure by family, friends, or community did not taint an admission of guilt. And some state legislatures modified the rule to allow confessions obtained by official flattery or statements of hope, provided that there was corroborative evidence from other sources.[10]

Sparse records prevent sure knowledge of how *Warickshall* applied in the courtroom. Trial judges sometimes accepted confessions gained by individuals other than law officers. When a local resident denied stealing a large sum of money from the state canal commissioners, for example, townspeople in one midwestern state extracted a confession by "application of Lynch's celebrated law." The suspect went to prison. Appellate courts reversed convictions if the confession clearly resulted from an official threat, even one as seemingly innocuous as an arresting officer's promise that if the defendant did not confess he would pursue him "to the end of the law and put him through it." Still, the language of threat had to be unmistakable. Thus a warning that the suspect "had better own up" to the theft of three gold coins was not sufficiently strong to exclude the subsequent confession. Guided by uncertain standards, law officers often seized the opportunity to induce confessions by nonthreatening behaviors, such as trickery and deception. In Indianapolis, for example, a counterfeiter's admission of guilt was "procured by officers pretending to be accomplices." Courts had no problem accepting these confessions. Protection against self-incrimination applied to official threats or torture, not to surreptitious or deceitful behavior.[11]

Antebellum jurists were especially concerned with maintaining the integrity of due process against legislative interference. Criminal statutes frequently brushed against the limits of what was permissible under state constitutional protection of rights of the accused. Exercising their power of judicial review, state supreme courts voided statutes that violated procedural safeguards and, in so doing, established definitions of due process that would resonate in U. S. Supreme Court decisions of the twentieth century.

Laws that attempted to enforce moral order often ran afoul of constitutional strictures, in part because, unlike crimes against persons or property, there was little public consensus on what constituted proper moral conduct, despite legislative pronouncements. Temperance legislation was especially controversial. To many reformers in the 1840s and 1850s, alcoholic beverages were the root cause of poverty, crime, and disease. When persuasion failed to lessen the flow of Demon Rum, temperance crusaders gained the passage of laws that prohibited or regulated wine, beer, and liquor. These laws frequently introduced novel law enforcement procedures, which opponents of prohibition challenged as unconstitutional violations of defendants' rights.

Like numerous other states, Massachusetts passed a prohibition law that allowed sheriffs, upon receipt of a warrant, to search premises they suspected of manufacturing or housing liquor. The owner, if known to the sheriff, would appear before a magistrate, who would conduct a hearing. Should the owner fail to appear or if the magistrate found him guilty, the liquor would be declared forfeit and destroyed.

When the Massachusetts supreme court heard the case of *Fisher* v. *McGirr* (1854), Chief Justice Lemuel Shaw, one of the great antebellum jurists, found that the prohibition law violated Article XIV of the Declaration of Rights, which secured citizens against unreasonable searches and seizures. Shaw conceded that the state had authority to control this form of property, but not through the use of a general warrant that gave sheriffs unrestricted power to search unspecified property for contraband items. The statute was subversive of a broad range of defendants' rights: it allowed proceedings without an indictment; it did not permit the defendant to face his accusers or to compel testimony; it omitted jury trial and even destroyed property upon the mere absence of the defendant, which in these proceedings constituted an admission of guilt. Shaw did not doubt that trial judges would follow due process, even without a legal prescription. But he concluded that the rights at stake were too fundamental to trust to the goodwill of magistrates or others. Criminal laws must be interpreted strictly: "the rights of parties ought not to be made to depend on a doubtful interpretation of various, and in some respects, incompatible and conflicting provisions." Constitutional guarantees of rights, he admonished, were "absolutely necessary to preserve the advantages of liberty, and maintain a free government."[12]

Judges were not the sole heirs to the legacy of the Bill of Rights. Nor were appellate cases the only avenue for defining those rights or for outlining what the safeguards meant for other social policies. State criminal codes, the law of crimes enacted by the legislature, also reflected the revolutionary heritage and influenced, at times indirectly, the antebellum understanding of rights.

One of the most striking developments in criminal justice was a shift in the center of law. Post-revolutionary criminal codes moved sharply away from colonial emphasis on morality to an increasing concern with the protection of private property and the security of private transactions. Prior to the Civil War, the United States was evolving into a complex, interdependent economy based on private ownership of property, entrepreneurial initiative, creative use of money and credit, and free movement of goods. Criminal law became another means to protect burgeoning capitalism. The rapid expansion in the number of economic crimes and heightened penalties attached to their violation represented a significant change in a criminal law previously focused on the detection and punishment of sin.[13]

Some changes in the criminal law addressed directly the practical meaning of revolutionary ideas. What, for example, was cruel and unusual punishment, the pregnant phrase found in the Eight Amendment and in all the state consitutions? Few legal issues have consumed as much emotional energy as the attempt to identify constitutionally permissible punishments, perhaps because punishment reveals so clearly the social function of criminal law. The experience of the early republic not only foreshadowed the controversies of the twentieth century, but it also revealed how long-standing is the tension between retribution and reformation in modern criminal justice.

The Italian reformer Cesare Beccaria had taught that the very severity of law made it necessary for criminals "to commit additional crimes to avoid punishment for a single one."[14] Americans of the revolutionary generation took this lesson to heart and set out to eliminate the excesses of colonial codes. Capital and corporal punishments were the most obvious targets for reform. Increased use of the death penalty throughout the British empire had not deterred crime, but it had inflamed the sensibilities of enlightened men and women. By replacing inhumane features of the legal system with rational laws and salutary punishments, reformers believed that crime could be controlled more effectively, if not actually decreased.[15]

Early opposition to the death penalty drew upon intellectual currents and experiences that extended far beyond Beccaria. Republican success depended upon virtuous citizens and voluntary consent to law. At the very least, this reliance on republican manners and opinions required that people abandon the habits and postures of corrupt monarchies. An especially vulgar tendency of such tyrannies was indiscriminate use of the gallows. "Capital punishments," wrote Benjamin Rush, a signer of the Declaration of Independence and the most prominent physician of his day, "are the natural offspring of monarchical governments." The very act of execution appealed not to man's higher instincts but to his passion. It also caused spectators to sympathize with the condemned and, in turn, to disdain the law. Even the conservative Alexander Hamilton agreed that "the idea of cruelty inspires disgust." The death penalty eroded rather than bolstered republican values and behavior.[16]

The 1780s and 1790s witnessed numerous remonstrances against both the terrible finality of the death penalty and its inability to deter crime. Home to the most active reformers were the New England states and

Pennsylvania. These states also housed the liberal theologies of Quakerism, Unitarianism, and Universalism, each of which emphasized the goodness of God and the redemptive possibilities for man. "A religion which commands us to forgive and even do good to our enemies," the Quaker Rush argued, "can never authorise the punishment of murder by death." Not every religious group agreed. More evangelical denominations invoked biblical authority for their position that eternal salvation did not depend upon a person's reformed behavior. But even if religion sanctioned the death penalty, opponents of capital punishment countered, such an extreme measure did not deter criminal behavior.[17]

Experience demonstrated that, in practice, society considered the punishments unduly harsh. William Bradford, attorney general and later supreme court justice for Pennsylvania during the post-revolutionary decades, reported to the state legislature in 1793 that juries frequently would not convict defendants charged with capital crimes and that many condemned felons ultimately received pardons. In both instances the result was the same: guilty men escaped the law's terrible power, thus blunting any deterrent effect that an execution might have. Even when men died for their crimes, any message about the consequences of evil was lost on a crowd of spectators who treated the occasion more like a carnival than a solemn rite.[18]

The death penalty, at least as practiced in the colonial period, was incompatible with republicanism, but if death was no longer a legitimate punishment, how would society control crime? One answer was the penitentiary, a new institution uniquely suited to the young republic. In 1786 Pennsylvania restricted capital punishment to cases of treason, murder, rape, and arson, a list that other states quietly adopted during the next two decades. Imprisonment at hard labor replaced death for all other felonies. By 1796 Virginia and New York joined the drift toward penitentiary confinement for most felonies. Within the next few decades, almost every state in the union would follow suit.[19]

Penitentiary: the word itself symbolized the hopes of reformers and signified the extent to which they had gone beyond Europeans who emphasized deterrence, not reformation, as the reason for prisons. Central to this new penology was the environmentalist psychology of the seventeenth-century English philosopher, John Locke, at least as it was understood in the new world. If environment molded character, as Locke argued, then would not confinement shelter offenders from evil companions and allow them to restore the decency that existed in all people? Such an egalitarian sentiment appealed to Americans. "We know that there are in every man," wrote South Carolinian Robert Turnbull, "even in the most hardened offenders, some few sparks of honour, a certain consciousness of the intrinsic nature of moral goodness, which though they be latent and apparently extinguished, yet may at any time be kindled and roused into action by the application of proper stimulus." The only question was what setting best accomplished this purpose.[20]

No penitentiary worked as outlined. Inadequate funding blunted plans to segregate prisoners, and by the 1820s and 1830s resistance to increased taxes led many states to contract with private individuals to house and supervise the convicts in exchange for their labor. Contract management often defeated attempts at reform. Profit, not repentance, was the goal of the private supervisor, and brutal treatment of the prisoners was too frequently the means used to secure their work. Giving the keeper "an interest in the proceeds of the labour of convicts leads to overworking and to treatment abhorrent to humane feelings," an Indiana newspaper concluded in 1845. More troubling, other critics argued, was that prisons were notorious schools for crime where "the ingenious and innocent . . . [are] thrown into the society of the dissipated and the depraved."[21]

The failure of the penitentiary doomed renewed attempts to abolish the death penalty. Throughout the nation the 1840s marked the zenith of the antebellum movement to remove execution from the list of acceptable sanctions. Abolition occurred only in Michigan and Wisconsin; in other states private executions replaced the spectacle of public hangings. Continued opposition to capital punishment depended less on republican ideology—this philosophy lost much of its significance after the War of 1812—than it did on growing egalitarian and individualistic strains in American culture. It is no coincidence that abolitionists of slavery and opponents of the death penalty shared the same platform and, indeed, were often the same people. But the campaign against the gallows faltered because lawmakers, and the voters they represented, were pessimistic about the possibilities for penitent reform. Popular fears of an increase in crime, a concern that coincided with the rapid development of cities and a spurt in non-English immigration, persuaded state legislatures that constitutional injunctions against cruel and unusual punishments did not extend to executions, especially when, compared to earlier decades, it applied to so few crimes.[22]

Reform did not begin and end with the campaign to create an acceptable system of punishment. Indeed, it is difficult to find an area of antebellum society untouched by the sentiment for improvement, if not perfection. Even the ancient institutions of the grand and petit jury, traditional bulwarks of liberty, became the object of reformers who sought to reconcile them with the new and triumphant democracy.

The first half of the nineteenth century witnessed numerous attempts to reform or even abolish the grand jury. Three issues—the jury's expense, inconvenience, and inefficiency—framed the debate, but underlying these concerns was a continuing discussion on the relationship between criminal justice, the nation's republican heritage, and its increasingly democratic future. To its proponents, the grand jury was an essential instrument in the battle to protect political liberty, defined in the older language of republicanism as the maintenance of public order and the promotion of public virtue. Opponents, who favored a system of public examination and presentment by a prosecutor before a magistrate, viewed the jury's secrecy as a threat to individual liberty in an open democratic society.

Grand juries performed a variety of functions in the nineteenth century. In theory, the grand jury was a representative local body that oversaw government officials and shielded citizens from overzealous and arbitrary prosecution. Jurors approved indictments of persons accused of crimes, inquired into the condition of roads and jails, investigated highway supervisors and tavern owners, and commented on any matter of concern to them or the community. But the experience of the early republic belied this rather benign theory. Federalist judges in the 1790s used their charges to the panel for partisan diatribes against Jeffersonians, giving credence to the anti-jury campaign of English philosopher Jeremy Bentham, who attacked the secrecy and inefficiency with which jurors, a "miscellaneous company of men," wielded power to the harm of liberty.

Early efforts to reform the grand jury focused on restrictions of its power to conduct political examinations. In his codification of Louisiana law in 1821, Edward Livingston limited judges to statements of law when addressing grand juries and confined jurors to ratifying only those indictments submitted to them. These provisions gained general acceptance, but other voices soon carried the reform beyond a restriction on the jury's unbridled power of inquiry to the concept of the jury itself. By 1850, an important American law journal, *The United States Monthly Law Magazine,* was urging that American lawyers and jurists follow their British counterparts and campaign for the abolition of the panel. At the same time, constitutional conventions in three midwestern states—Michigan, Ohio, and Indiana—entertained various proposals to eliminate the jury, with the Indiana Constitution of 1851 permitting the legislature to take such action.[23]

The assault on the grand jury stemmed from perceptions that it was inefficient and undemocratic, characteristics that ran counter to demands for open but limited government. Critics judged the institution to be costly and unproductive. Too many of its indictments failed upon prosecution, wasting taxpayers' money and inconveniencing witnesses, petty jurors, and other participants. Worse, the jury was undemocratic. It conducted a secret inquiry and considered only testimony that supported an indictment. The *ex parte* or one-sided nature of the jury's investigation encouraged vindictive prosecutions and tarnished an indicted person's reputation, no matter how much the law presumed innocence. And too often bystanders at court—loafers and drunkards, opponents claimed—filled the panel, thus defeating the body's representativeness.

Supporters of the jury responded by evoking the institution's history as a bulwark against tyranny. They defended secrecy as a means of promoting rational deliberation, insulated from public pressure, and of ensuring an unbridled investigation into wrongdoing, from whatever corner. Placing the authority to prosecute in one or two officials concentrated power too much and offered no protection for liberty. No one invoked the provisions of the Fifth Amendment in the jury's defense—the Amendment applied only to the federal government—but few advocates of the jury left in doubt their conviction that this local institution was essential to due process.

Grand jury reform failed, at least in the short term. The concerns voiced by opponents were not sufficiently pronounced to override traditional images of the grand jury as a protector of individual liberty. But the debate simply waned; it did not disappear. Later in the nineteenth century the assault on the grand jury would emerge with greater force—and this time with more success. Fears of urban crime and the perceived disorder of foreign immigration would strengthen the demand for more efficient and effective law enforcement, even if this meant redefining what due process required.[24]

The petit jury also came under increasing attack during the antebellum decades, although for different reasons. Under common law, jurors exercised authority by a general verdict, innocent or guilty, given in response to a defendant's plea to a criminal charge. This verdict merged law and fact, that is, it represented the jury's judgment on what happened (fact) and whether the act was illegal (law). The general verdict enabled jurors to fit the law to local circumstances. In theory, a jury declared guilt only when the facts proved at trial matched, beyond a reasonable doubt, the provisions of the law defining the crime. But the jury did not have to explain or defend its decision. Did a verdict of not guilty mean that the accused was innocent or merely that his actions were no crime to his neighbors, regardless of what the law stated? Jurors did not operate totally without restraint. Trial judges could exclude irrelevant evidence, instruct jurors on matters of the law, although the jury was not bound to accept the instruction, and arrest judgment or declare a mistrial. Yet prior to 1800 there were few challenges to the jury's authority to decide the facts and to choose whether or not the law applied. An unfettered jury served the ends of justice well, at least as defined by local standards.

A new relationship between judge and jury emerged in the nineteenth century as judges repudiated the notion that juries could determine law in criminal cases. The change was gradual. Early courts upheld an unvarnished jury power. Not until 1845, when the Massachusetts supreme court rigidly defined separate roles for the judge and jury, did state courts begin to move away from hitherto unquestioned jury discretion to decide the criminal law. Fears of majoritarian tyranny, a desire to ensure uniform justice, and a recognition that an unlimited jury boded ill for judicial power combined to produce a new maxim: the judge decides in matters of law; the jury in matters of fact. More stringent rules for the admission of evidence, the ability to set aside verdicts contrary to the evidence, and the right of the state to appeal the decision were important corollaries of this principle. Even attempts to make the jury's law-deciding power part of state constitutional law did not dam for long the mid-nineteenth century shift to increased judicial authority in criminal trials.[25]

These developments did not impair the right to a trial by jury, at least not directly. Nor did they mean an immediate and irreversible diminishment of the community's role in criminal justice. Antebellum criminal process was too decentralized and too dependent on citizen participation through such institutions as the grand and petit juries to maintain much distance from local concerns. And the election of judges, which occurred for trial courts in the 1820s and extended to the appellate bench by the 1850s, undoubtedly slowed the shift of authority in the courtroom and kept criminal justice closely tied to the community.

Other developments gradually outweighed the dominant local influence on criminal law. The bar became better educated, more professional, and greater attuned to other-than-local events and ideas. Manifested politically through an emphasis on equality, intellectual opinion trumpeted the desirability of more uniform decisions, a result facilitated by the widely available publication of state appellate reports and the appearance for the first time of major American treatises on criminal law, exemplified by the work of Joel P. Bishop. The codification movement, an effort to systematize and rationalize the common law, although unsuccessful, exalted a more scientific approach to law that further distanced it from local influence. Regardless of the impulses that governed these various developments, the result was often the same: justice began to achieve a more universal, less local, definition.[26]

Yet always the administration of justice was local in origin, and since most defendants did not appeal a conviction, its local dominance went unchallenged in practice. It was in the trial court and in the county jail that the theory of rights became real for most defendants. Here too criminal process reflected the social and intellectual changes that had guided reforms of the institutions of justice, although tradition and custom sometimes muted the effect of these larger influences.

The machinery of law enforcement in antebellum America changed rapidly and in ways that affected significantly the rights granted defendants in practice. Poorly paid and ill-trained police replaced nightwatchmen in emerging cities. Partisanship, not professionalism, characterized these early forces. In many cities, political hacks dominated the officer ranks, and patrolmen were drawn from the party faithful. Created to protect property and, to a lesser extent, persons from the disorder thought to be endemic in cities, their job was to control the urban mob and arrest criminals, by whatever means and force were necessary. Few people held policemen responsible for protecting rights of the accused: defendants' rights began in the courts, not in the streets. In this attitude, city police differed little from the country sheriff, who remained the most visible local symbol of law enforcement. Both urban police and rural sheriffs reflected the antebellum creed of limited government and low taxes.[27]

For much of the antebellum period, the structure and function of criminal justice mirrored practices of a much earlier time. Circuit courts headed by trial judges usually handled serious misdemeanors and all felonies, but justices of the peace were often the defendants' first contact with the criminal process. These popularly elected minor officials continued in their traditional roles of county supervisors and examining judges. Chosen for their political skills or reputation, justices had only limited knowledge of the law and learned much of what they knew from other justices or from one of several widely distributed manuals of forms and procedures. Not surprisingly, lawyer-dominated legislatures gradually restricted their jurisdiction to minor breaches of the peace and petty theft. Only urban justices in municipal courts, often called mayor's or police courts, experienced any expansion of power to try offenders. Still, justices were important to the criminal process. They retained the authority to make preliminary inquiries into alleged crimes and to bind suspects and witnesses over to the grand jury for indictment. Except for serious crimes, they did not require bail from the accused but simply released them on personal recognizance, that is, a promise to appear before the grand jury if called.[28]

Prosecution of crime in the early republic often depended upon the initiative of the victim or his kin. State prosecutors existed but their official duties were usually limited to presenting cases to the grand jury, drawing up the indictment, and managing the state's case at trial. Circuit-riding made this stance necessary. The court's jurisdiction usually extended over several counties, with the judge, prosecutor, and practicing attorneys moving to each county seat for a week or so until the term was over. Frequently arriving on Sunday for Monday's opening of court, prosecutors spent the first few days with the grand jury, while the judge tried civil cases. Because of the low salary and high demands, turnover among prosecutors was high. But attorneys hired by the victim or his family could also join the case, forming a prosecutorial team of public and private counsel. This practice permitted a stronger presentation of the state's case and, equally important, tied notions of justice more closely to community norms than to an abstract standard.[29]

Criminal trials occurred in a flurry of activity on the last few days of the session. Seven or eight trials in a single day were not unusual as judges tried to avoid continuing cases to the next term. Most defendants for serious crimes had counsel, either of their own choosing or appointed by the court at public expense. A surprising number of defendants decided to plead guilty, foregoing a trial before their peers in the expectation of receiving a lighter sentence from the judge. This practice, often called implicit bargaining by modern scholars, probably came at the suggestion of counsel and was a precursor of the system of plea bargaining that developed later in the century. Frequently the decision to admit guilt was a wise one. Courts were notoriously inefficient in prosecuting crime— early national Virginia, for example, discharged one-third of defendants before trial—but cases carried to conclusion, especially for serious crimes, had a high conviction rate. Most states, however, did not devote sufficient resources to the legal system to permit a highly effective criminal prosecution, nor did society make this a priority, despite complaints about the increase in crime.[30]

Due process in these antebellum courts was no hollow ideal. Trial judges took seriously their responsibility to do justice without fear or favor. Judge James Doty, circuit judge in the Michigan Territory in the 1820s, was typical of his peers in more settled areas. He studied the law religiously, keeping up with decisions elsewhere and applying common-law principles to new and uncharted situations. Even when faced with continuing pressure by white settlers to aid their grab for land, Doty's careful notes reveal that he extended every procedural guarantee to the natives, even allowing Indian witnesses before his court to subscribe to an oath that swore by a great spirit other than the Christian God.[31]

With certain exceptions, notably blacks, there is little evidence to suggest that state and local governments made blatant or systematic use of criminal law to suppress unpopular groups or individuals. It is also true that certain people were more susceptible to the demands of law than others. Ethnic groups, religious minorities, and always the poor were prominent among offenders but underrepresented in the jurybox or on the bench. The apparent paradox is easier to explain than to understand: antebellum Americans defined due process almost exclusively in pro-cedural terms. Their belief in proper form excluded the possibility that strict adherence to procedures could lead to a denial of justice.

Ironically, the criminal law of slavery reveals most clearly the central role of due process in American jurisprudence. Slavery was in theory and practice a local institution, supported by codes that fixed the status and responsibilities of masters and slaves alike. These codes defined slaves as personal property or "chattels personal" and made the power of the master over them absolute. But the laws also recognized that slaves were human beings who could exercise their will in ways that threatened white society. Lawmakers uniformly prescribed more severe punishments for blacks, slave or free, than for whites convicted of the same crime. The death penalty, under contraction elsewhere in the law, awaited slaves who murdered in any degree or who robbed, poisoned, rebelled against, or raped whites. Codes became more harsh as sectional tension over slavery mounted and as southern states experienced uprisings or threats that challenged the legitimacy or authority of the slave system.[32]

The slave codes differed radically from Anglo-American legal traditions. Yet southerners were also heir to republican ideals, including its reverence for individual rights and the rule of law, and southern judges were articulate and forceful advocates of due process within the common-law tradition. Southern legislatures and especially the region's appellate bench were surprisingly respectful of a slave's procedural rights in serious criminal cases. Georgia in 1850 extended full procedural equality to slaves, and a Florida judge in 1860 proudly proclaimed "that whenever life is involved, the slave stands upon as safe ground as the master."[33]

Such rhetoric was overdrawn, intended to demonstrate to northerners the fairness of southern justice. It was also misleading, although not by as much as contemporary critics maintained. Slaves had access to a wide range of procedural rights, including counsel appointed by the court, and available records suggest that defending lawyers took their responsibilities seriously. But the guarantees applied only because they threatened neither the southern economy nor its system of racial control.[34]

The requirement of due process in slave trials masked the inherent injustice of slavery. Still, its very presence reveals just how powerfully rooted in American law was the notion that justice demanded fair and impartial procedures. Southern jurists were not acting out some charade by insisting that the state follow prescribed procedures when trying accused slaves. These judges could conceive of the law's operation in no other way. Due process was too fundamental to the law itself, even in a code that denied liberty.

The antebellum decades ended in a wave of constitutional reform.

Swept by democratic fervor and shaken by the economic instability of the 1830s and 1840s, voters in state after state approved new constitutions with detailed provisions that were legislative in nature, rather than organic. Legislative authority declined, executive power increased, and judges, both trial and appellate, became elected officials. Jacksonian reforms also found expression in the fundamental law, including such penal innovations as the penitentiary and separate "houses of refuge" for juvenile and women offenders.[35]

One thing that did not change in the new constitutions was the canon of rights that defined due process for the accused. The language used to identify these rights mimicked the phrases of the federal amendments and earlier state documents. Much had changed in the half-century or more since the ratification of the Bill of Rights, however. Americans still venerated the concept of due process and attributed much of their liberty to its protection. But its guarantees were ones of procedural fairness only. Some of the institutions most closely linked to these safeguards, such as the grand and petit jury, had come under increasing attack. The extension of popular democracy, and especially its definition as majoritarian rule, posed as yet an ill-defined challenge to the rule of law. The persecution of unpopular minorities—for example, the Mormons—and the paradoxical existence of due process within slave codes suggested that procedural guarantees offered scant protection to individuals who existed on society's fringes or who were not part of an economic, social, or political majority.

The United States at mid-century prided itself on free and open government within a democratic society. Sustaining this democracy was a strong egalitarianism that insisted on universal standards, a sentiment, ironically, that acted in coming decades to defeat the local control of government that had, in the American understanding, restrained official power. Uniform justice, an enviable ideal, conflicted sharply with the persistent localism of American culture and over time eroded traditional conceptions of justice, including due process. After the Civil War, the stresses placed on criminal justice would reveal just how inadequate the antebellum framework was in safeguarding liberty in an increasing industrial and polyglot age.

4

THE MEANING OF DUE PROCESS, 1865–1930

In January 1859, a deputy sheriff from Marion County, Indiana, arrested James A. McCorkle in San Antonio, Texas, and secured his extradition on a charge of stealing funds from his Indianapolis employer. At his first trial, the jury deadlocked after deliberating for two days, and the judge declared a mistrial. Later in the term McCorkle again faced a jury, despite his protest that the new trial was a violation of his constitutional protection against double jeopardy.

The second trial began on Wednesday but had proceeded only as far as empanelling a jury before the new trial judge, Justice Samuel Perkins of the state supreme court, adjourned for the day. That night McCorkle escaped jail. Thursday morning, defense counsel Jacob and George W. Julian, soon to achieve prominence as a Republican senator, asked Perkins "to discharge the jury and terminate the trial." The judge refused, whereupon the Julians walked out in protest "against the strange proceeding of trying a man for life or liberty in his absence." With newly appointed attorneys, the trial continued as if the defendant were present. By Friday afternoon, McCorkle had been returned to the courtroom. Two hours later the jury returned a verdict of guilty. The sentence: four years in the state prison.

An appeal proved futile. The supreme court, in an opinion written by Perkins, also the trial judge, acknowledged that both the state constitution and statute law provided that trial could not occur in the defendant's absence. Decisions from other jurisdictions supported this rule. But in this instance, the court claimed, the defendant had waived his right to be present. McCorkle's escape and the withdrawal of his counsel undoubtedly prejudiced the jury's consideration of the case, Perkins admitted. This result did not bother the justice: "The consequences were definitely sought . . . ; they should now be silently borne."

Public comment on the case supported the decision. "The law, or at least judicial construction, has long leaned against society, and in favor of the accused parties," the *Indiana Daily Journal* wrote. "[I]t is time that the balance was restored between Justice and Mercy, and the safety of society regarded as much as the technical rights of criminals. . . . It is time community had a share of the regards of Courts, and that occasional constructions and rulings be directed to some other purpose than helping criminals to evade the penalties of their crimes."[1]

McCorkle v. *State* was a minor case; it established no great principle of constitutional or criminal law. Still, the decision startles the student of antebellum jurisprudence. It reflects little of the concern for rights of the accused that had been present in American political thought, at least formally, since the drafting of the Bill of Rights. But it foreshadowed a revolution in criminal justice, one that made administrative efficiency, not rights, the touchstone of law.

Changes came first in trial courts. Under the influence of a new, scientific criminology, courts adopted innovations such as plea bargaining and bench trial that, in practice, circumvented unpredictable juries and made punishment more certain. Statute law also responded to new theories. In many states an information, a formal accusation drafted by the prosecutor alone, substituted for grand jury indictment as the method of commencing prosecution, and indeterminate sentences replaced fixed terms in an effort to make the punishment fit the criminal rather than the crime. Other changes were more subtle. The role of police expanded, professional bureaucrats began to staff the system, and administrative requirements of efficiency and universal standards of justice redefined the community's role in legal process.

Appellate opinions and legal treatises did not retreat from a formal concern for due process. Changes in criminal justice were often subterranean and sometimes not even apparent to individuals who worked inside the courts or station houses. Judges and legal theorists rarely confronted the meaning of new developments; they infrequently questioned whether new practices denied an accused person the protection intended by constitutional guarantees. Focus shifted from proper techniques of charging an individual with a crime to questions of what evidence would be permitted, but in both instances the approach to issues was mechanical, involving proper form and timing rather than substance. Not until the Progressive era was there any sustained discussion of what impact various changes in criminal justice had on traditional conceptions of due process.

The changes in criminal process came in response to new social and economic realities. In many ways, the latter half of the nineteenth century bears more resemblance to the twentieth century than it does to pre-war decades. It was an industrial age: within three generations after the Civil War, the United States had become the world's greatest manufacturing nation. Much of this growth was attributable to new consumer or industrial products that today are commonplace—telephones, steel, oil, electricity, automobiles. It was also an urban age: in 1860, only one in five people lived in towns of 2,500 or more; by 1920, the figure had swelled to include half of the nation's population. Growth came from two sources: a farm-to-city migration spurred by the mechanization of agriculture and a sharp rise in the number of immigrants, especially from eastern and southern Europe and Asia.

Optimism, pride, and even arrogance accompanied the new order; so did discontent, protest, fear, and anxiety. Wealth increased in spectacular fashion, yet economic growth followed an uneven course, with major depressions in the 1870s and 1890s and frequent downturns every few years. Despite a large and prosperous middle class, the extremes of wealth and poverty had never been more obvious. Workers were poorly paid, especially those in unskilled or semiskilled occupations, and working conditions were often dangerous to life or health. Owners and managers resisted labor's attempts to organize, resulting in industrial riots and violent clashes between the two groups. Cities often appeared ungovernable as rapid growth outstripped the delivery of urban services. More troublesome was the metropolis' tendency to harbor the so-called "dangerous classes," those "great masses of the destitute, miserable, and criminal persons" who, according to social reformer Charles Loring Brace in 1872, lurked "hidden beneath the surface of society."[2]

A search for order consumed the energies of nineteenth-century lawmakers and reformers. Nowhere was the desire for stability and control more apparent than in the nation's criminal justice systems. The plural is appropriate because the United States was still a nation of states. The strict antebellum separation of state and central power did not disappear with the Civil War, although the somewhat redundant term "dual federalism" gave it a new veneer. In one of the great ironies of American history, most constitutional theorists, including a majority of justices on the U. S. Supreme Court, pretended that the Union victory made no permanent changes in the essential relationship between states and the central government. There were exceptions, of course, but in matters of criminal process states retained almost exclusive control.[3]

The Supreme Court's reluctance to extend the Bill of Rights to the states was not because of lack of opportunity, nor did it stem from a lack of concern with the traditional guarantees of due process. Unprecedented economic development in the decades following the war spurred a tremendous expansion of federal criminal law, especially in areas tied to constitutionally delegated powers such as taxation, interstate commerce, and the postal system. Reconstruction policies protecting the civil rights of recently freed blacks also required more federal involvement in criminal justice. Inevitably, federal prosecution tested the limits of the constitutional protections of defendants' rights. With few exceptions, the Supreme Court proved to be a worthy, if cautious, guardian of these guarantees.

The first tests of criminal due process came during and immediately after the outbreak of war. As early as April 1861 pro-secession mobs in northern cities forcibly contested the passage of Union troops, and in border states southern sympathizers recruited and trained armed volunteers for the Confederacy. The law of treason was too muddy to permit confident prosecution of such activity, and state criminal statutes were irrelevant. In response to the crisis, President Lincoln, claiming extraordinary emergency powers, suspended the writ of habeas corpus and ordered the arrest and detention of persons "dangerous to the public safety." Often without sufficient evidence to make a definite charge, military authorities, federal marshals, and secret service agents detained hundreds of suspected subversives until the immediate emergency passed. Civilian judges frequently sought the release of such prisoners, but military officers disregarded their orders.[4]

Most constitutional scholars have long since vindicated Lincoln, but Roger B. Taney, Chief Justice of the U. S. Supreme Court in 1861, was not so accommodating. Taney was a Maryland slaveowner who had outraged many northerners with his tortured opinion denying Negro citizenship in *Dred Scott* v. *Sanford* (1857). Now the Chief Justice was ready to challenge the President. When military authorities arrested fellow Marylander and Confederate recruiter, James B. Merryman, and imprisoned him as a threat to internal security, Taney ordered his release on a writ of habeas corpus, a mandate that Lincoln rejected. In his opinion, drafted in the capacity as judge over the federal circuit that included Maryland but delivered in the posture of Chief Justice, Taney claimed that Congress alone had the power to suspend the writ of habeas corpus. Not only was Lincoln's executive order unconstitutional, Taney implied, but it deprived Americans of one of the chief guarantees of their liberty, protection against arbitrary arrest.[5]

Taney adopted a standard gloss on the writ, but his protest was politically motivated and misleading. Federal habeas writs had been insignificant as a protection of unjust imprisonment, primarily because the roster of federal crimes was so small. State habeas was the important guarantee in criminal trials. Popularly elected state judges were often unwilling to employ the writ against state or local officials, and federal judges deferred to state jurisdiction in criminal cases involving a violation of state law. Thus, most defendants had no effective redress except appeal against unjust criminal proceedings. The writ, for all practical purposes, was irrelevant everywhere, a circumstance that suited the states-rights' nationalism of the Chief Justice.[6]

Lincoln ignored Taney's protests and continued to suspend the writ of habeas corpus in areas where resistance to the war effort threatened Union victory. Finally in 1863 Congress passed the Habeas Corpus Act, authorizing these suspensions as provided in Article I, Section 9 of the Constitution. The act was a recognition that preservation of the Union justified Lincoln's extreme measures. But it also required the release of political prisoners if grand juries found no indictments against them. Even wartime emergency could not justify a complete abandonment of this vital element of due process; judicial procedures once again became the basis for detention of prisoners.

More important, the act signaled a greatly expanded role for federal courts in criminal process, an area previously left exclusively to state jurisdiction. Prior to the war, criminal justice was overwhelmingly local, both in theory and practice. Even when alleging an infringement of a federal constitutional right, defendants could gain relief only on a writ of error to the U. S. Supreme Court. No federal court could intervene in pre-trial maneuvering or shift trial from state to federal jurisdiction. The

Habeas Corpus Act established a new practice and rested it on an emerging conviction that rights could not be left solely to the protection of state courts. Through the agency of the federal courts, there now existed the possibility of national standards of justice.[7]

Due process and the federal courts' role in its enforcement were also much at issue in the most important constitutional development of the postwar Reconstruction, the nationalization of civil rights under the Thirteenth and Fourteenth Amendments. The Thirteenth Amendment, ratified in December 1865, abolished slavery and gave Congress the power to enforce the prohibition by appropriate legislation, thus completing the process that had begun with the Emancipation Proclamation (1863). The federal government now had authority over personal liberty, a power previously reserved exclusively to the states. But did the amendment bestow any civil rights on ex-slaves, and if so, how would those rights be enforced? Congress could not agree on the answer to this question. Only in 1866, when it became apparent that newly enacted "Black Codes" in the southern states imposed a second-class citizenship and, in some instances, partial bondage on former slaves did Congress adopt the Civil Rights Act to protect the liberty and rights of freed blacks.[8]

The act challenged prevailing conceptions of due process and federal-state power. It defined state and national citizenship as essentially the same and opened federal tribunals to individuals unable to enforce their rights of citizenship in state courts. This latter provision implied that Congress could assume the power of local police and criminal law, traditionally a power reserved exclusively to the states. Citing its unconstitutionality, President Johnson objected to the bill, but Congress swiftly overrode his veto.[9]

Sufficient doubts existed about the act to spur passage of another amendment, the Fourteenth, that would remove any constitutional objections. The amendment included a citizenship clause making all native-born or naturalized persons citizens of both the United States and their state of residence. More important was the guarantee of civil rights contained in Section 1: "No state shall make or enforce any law which shall abridge the privileges and immunities of citizens of the United States; nor shall any state deprive any person of life, liberty, or property, without due process of law; nor deny to any person within its jurisdiction equal protection of the laws."

The language proved to be pregnant with meaning for rights of the accused—in the twentieth century. But as interpreted by the Supreme Court during the late nineteenth century, the amendment maintained only a tenuous connection with the events and ideas that gave it birth. The Fourteenth Amendment nationalized civil rights: the national government guaranteed to its citizens the protection of rights under the Constitution. And since national and state citizenship was the same, it also gave the federal courts supervisory authority over personal liberty and civil rights, previously the responsibility of state governments alone. Yet federal guarantees proved hollow in the area of criminal justice because few people believed that the amendment modified the states' almost exclusive control of criminal process.[10]

The amendment reflected a changing definition of civil rights, one that arose from wartime experiences, and a new understanding of the federal government's role in protecting these rights. Civil rights meant substantially less in the 1860s than they do today. The term referred to a free person's ability to enter into contracts, to sue or be sued, to choose a profession, or to engage in any other private action, usually economic in nature, without obstruction by the state or private citizens. State and local law gave shape to rights enjoyed by free persons. Communities could permit or forbid certain activities, relationships, or remedies, and in doing so expand or restrict the list of civil rights. In reality, rights were merely the privileges of citizenship. As such, the state could not discriminate against individual citizens who exercised rights granted to all free men, nor could it legitimately fail to protect rights against private interference.[11]

Prior to the amendment, national civil rights had been relatively few compared to the limitless privileges conferred by state citizenship. The Bill of Rights protected individuals against actions of the federal government, but not against state or private acts. Yet the war and Reconstruction had proven that southern state governments especially, either by legislation such as the Black Codes or non-enforcement of criminal laws, posed the biggest threat to civil rights of ex-slaves, the nation's newest citizens. The Fourteenth Amendment, by equating state and national citizenship, created an endless list of national civil rights and, more important, made the central government responsible for protecting them.

Did the amendment mean that the Bill of Rights now acted as a restraint upon states as well as the federal government? In matters of criminal procedure, at least according to the Supreme Court, the answer was relatively simple: No. For most justices the basic tenets of federalism remained intact. State constitutions protected the rights of the accused. Surprisingly few cases tested the issue. In one that did, *Hurtado* v. *California* (1884), the Court ruled that the Fifth Amendment guarantee of a grand-jury indictment in criminal proceedings applied only to federal trials.[12] Whatever the intent of the framers of the amendment—and scholars have long and inconclusively debated the issue—the Court was unwilling to depart from the tradition that state governments were primarily responsible for the integrity of criminal due process.

The *Slaughterhouse Cases* (1873) set the pattern for the Court's interpretation of the amendment, at least until the 1890s. Justice Samuel F. Miller, for a 5–4 majority, rejected an appeal from white New Orleans butchers that a Louisiana law creating a monopoly in the slaughtering trade violated their rights as citizens under the Fourteenth Amendment because it deprived them of liberty and property without due process of law. The amendment, Miller argued, did not change the traditional nature of federalism. State and federal citizenship were essentially separate, and national citizenship conferred no rights outside of those that related to the individual's direct relationship to the federal government. Most rights belonging to Americans were attributes of state citizenship and thus were not subject to national regulation or control. Further, there was no infringement of due process. The state had followed proper legal procedures in granting the monopoly; it had not acted arbitrarily.[13]

Subsequent decisions affirmed traditional tenets of federalism and due process. Dual federalism was the new phrase that described an older notion that state and central government occupied separate spheres of authority which neither could overstep. Only overt state abridgement of civil rights permitted the federal government to intercede for the protection of citizens under the Fourteenth Amendment. Due process referred only to the procedures employed by the state. If criminal prosecutions followed the process required by law, then the result by definition was justice.

Even such limited supervisory authority had clear implications for rights of the accused, especially black defendants. State laws forbidding blacks to serve on juries violated the Fourteenth Amendment, the Court held, as did the action of a state court judge in excluding blacks from jury service. Silence of the state constitution or laws offered no exemption from the amendment's language, the Court ruled in another case. The actual practice of excluding black jurors also violated the constitutional protection. But almost in the same instant the justices decided that absence of Negroes from juries did not necessarily deny black defendants the right of judgment by their peers. As a practical matter, white officials could exclude blacks with impunity by exercising care in the selection process. Black voters simply would not appear on lists of potential jurors that county officials prepared for the court.[14]

Significantly, these decisions rested on the amendment's equal protection clause, not on an expanded definition of due process. But if the Court's majority failed to address the issue of due process, a minority of justices beginning with the *Slaughterhouse Cases* pressed for a much broader interpretation based on the result of state action and not just the procedures used to achieve it. Substantive due process, or the notion that justice depends upon a correct verdict as well as fair procedures, was not a radical idea. Its ideological progenitor was the concept of vested rights, the early nineteenth-century theory that certain rights belonged to an individual so completely that government was bound to protect them against any adverse action. These vested rights were almost always economic in nature and controversy over them centered on the exercise of monopoly powers. Holders of exclusive privileges, such as bridge owners who possessed sole right of passage across a river, believed their monopoly was immune from abridgement or regulation. Yet vested rights lost judicial favor in the 1830s when it became apparent the doctrine impeded technological progress.

The concept of substantive due process provided new dress for the discarded idea. Now, some rights in liberty and property were so fundamental government could not regulate them at all, even if it adopted the fairest possible procedure for doing so. Who determined which rights were inviolable, and who decided when they had been threatened? Judges, of course. The new doctrine implied that universal standards of justice existed, that judges, not legislatures or juries, defined them, and that laws or local actions leading to unfair results violated due process. Not only did this conception run counter to prevailing definitions of due process, it invited extensive federal judicial review of state and local conduct whenever defendants alleged an unfair result.[15]

The Court adopted standards of substantive due process by the 1890s, but only in cases involving state regulation of property or business interests. There was a paradox at work here. The Fourteenth Amendment meant more in an area, economic rights, not intended by its framers than it did in the realm, civil rights, most prominent in their minds. A majority of justices opposed to state interference with private or corporate economic decisions ruled in a series of opinions that, even when following all procedures established by the legislature, such regulation deprived the defendants of their property and thus failed to meet the tests of due process. Distrustful of popular majorities, the justices substituted their own notions of sound economic policy for those of elected representatives.[16]

The growth of big business and the emergence of the United States as a world power confirmed for many people the correctness of the doctrine— until the Great Depression of the 1930s created a demand for precisely the sort of regulation the Court had previously rejected. Substantive due process did not disappear from the nation's legal vocabulary; it simply acquired a new meaning in the mid-twentieth century when the Supreme Court applied the Fourteenth Amendment to non-economic state actions and transformed the amendment's due process clause into a substantive protection for a whole host of individual rights, including rights of the accused.

For many commentators and scholars, the demise of economic due process and its resurrection in different form as a guarantor of individual rights marks the beginning of the Bill of Rights' application to criminal process. Such a view is mistaken, even if one focuses entirely on the Supreme Court. On the whole, the Court hewed to the line drawn in civil rights cases that the Fourteenth Amendment imposed no obligation on states. But the expansion of federal criminal law in the decades following the Civil War brought before the justices a host of cases addressing the meaning of criminal due process and the constitutional protections afforded by the Fourth, Fifth, Sixth, and Eighth Amendments. Some cases set benchmark interpretations of the right in question, although many issues were of little significance except to the defendant. And a few of the cases, especially those that featured signal dissents by Justice John Marshall Harlan, foreshadowed later constitutional interpretation.

The scope of the Fourth Amendment's protection against warrantless searches and seizures was the issue in two opinions of great importance to criminal investigation and trial. Not only was the leading case, *Boyd* v. *United States* (1886), the first case of any consequence on the subject, it remains the boldest and most far-reaching opinion on the subject yet issued by the Court. Perhaps more than any other single case, *Boyd* rescued its controlling amendment from becoming, in the words of modern Justice William J. Brennan, "a dead letter in the federal courts."[17] It also set the stage for a subsequent decision, *Weeks* v. *United States* (1914), that announced one of the most controversial doctrines ever to stem from an amendment, the federal exclusionary rule.

For all of its constitutional importance, the *Boyd* case involved a trifling offense. Federal prosecutors alleged that George and Edward Boyd, New York City merchants, had imported thirty-five cases of glass duty-free in violation of customs laws. At trial, the district judge ordered the Boyds to produce the invoice for glass previously imported so the government could prove the worth of the cargo in question. The defendants, under protest, were compelled to produce evidence that convicted them. Was this an illegal search? Did compulsory process jeopardize the Boyd's protection against self-incrimination? These were the questions facing the Court.[18]

Justice Bradley's opinion for the Court revealed the liberal construction the justices were ready to grant rights of the accused. Case facts did not require a broad ruling. The trial was a civil proceeding—the government sought only recovery of the duty, not criminal penalties—and the Court earlier had ruled that Fourth Amendment protection extended only to criminal matters.[19] In addition, there was no physical search for evidence of crime and no attempt to seize contraband, so the word "search" required a new definition simply to fall under the prohibition. Bradley brushed aside these obstacles in a sweeping ruling. The Fourth Amendment protected individuals from actual searches and other procedures that sought to accomplish the effect of a search. The Constitution permitted searches only for contraband articles; any proceeding that sought mere evidence of crime was an unreasonable search and therefore illegal.

Then Bradley reached the most expansive feature of his opinion, one that subsequent cases would trim and modify. Despite their separate histories, the Fourth and Fifth Amendments defined each other: the prohibition against unreasonable searches was part of a broader right against self-incrimination, thus tying the Fourth Amendment doctrinally to the Fifth Amendment's promise that no person "shall be compelled in any criminal case to be a witness against himself." A warrantless seizure of evidence deprived the accused of the Fifth Amendment's protection. The reason for such an interpretation became clear in a closing passage that still commands respect: "[U]nconstitutional practices get their first footing . . . by silent approaches and slight deviations from legal modes of procedure. . . . It is the duty of courts to be watchful for the constitutional rights of the citizen, and guard against any stealthy encroachments thereon."[20]

This impassioned defense represented the high-water mark for the privilege, and it revealed that the Court did not construe constitutional rights of the accused casually. But the decision failed to address the pressing issue of enforcement. Trial courts were ineffective guards against an unreasonable search since it occurred during the stage of investigation and before judges even had knowledge of the matter. Compounding the problem was the common-law rule accepting illegally seized evidence, no matter how acquired, so long as it was trustworthy. The only available remedy, a private suit in tort against an individual officer, offered little or no protection against convictions gained through illegal searches. Under such a standard the Fourth Amendment could become a dead letter, no matter how tied to the privilege against self-incrimination. The solution was obvious: make illegally seized evidence inadmissible at trial.

The Court took this step in 1914 when, in *Weeks* v. *United States,* it broke with common-law precedent and ordered the exclusion from federal trials of evidence obtained through unconstitutional search. "If letters and private documents can thus be seized and held and used in evidence . . . the protection of the Fourth Amendment . . . is of no value," wrote Justice Day for the Court. Protection from crime "is not to be aided by the sacrifice of these great principles established by years of endeavor and suffering which have resulted in their embodiment in the fundamental law of the land."[21]

Weeks was a landmark decision, but its limitation was apparent. It did not apply to the states. If state or local police conducted the search and turned over otherwise illegally obtained evidence to federal officials, the evidence would be admissible. This practice, the so-called "silver platter" exception to the exclusionary rule, became a routine method of investigation for federal officials. The decision also meant that local prosecutors could introduce illegally seized evidence in trials under state law so long as the state constitution or laws allowed it, which most did.

The federal rule was not without effect because some states adopted it, but the vast majority of defendants were tried in jurisdictions where the common-law practice of admitting such evidence prevailed until 1961, when, in *Mapp* v. *Ohio,* the Court applied the exclusionary principle to all criminal trials, federal and state.[22]

In the 1920s the emergence of new technologies persuaded the Court to modify somewhat its ringing affirmation of Fourth Amendment rights. Criminals had discovered the great mobility offered by the automobile, especially in smuggling liquor. Federal agents began to conduct warrant-less searches of suspected bootlegger's cars, using the evidence seized to gain convictions under the Volstead Act, the national prohibition law. In *Carroll* v. *United States* (1925), the Court created an exception to the Fourth Amendment's requirement that no search and seizure take place without a warrant. The majority justified the automobile exception for practical reasons: time and circumstances rarely allowed law officers to obtain a warrant beforehand; if they waited for such approval, the car would be gone by the time a warrant arrived. But this exception, the Court warned, did not permit unlimited searches of all cars. No search, under warrant or warrantless, could be conducted without probable cause.[23]

Wire tapping also posed problems for the Court. The ability to listen covertly to the private conversations of suspected criminals proved attractive to the Federal Bureau of Investigation and other law enforcement agencies. Did the use of this new technology constitute a search or seizure under the meaning of the Fourth Amendment, thus requiring a warrant? No, the sharply divided (5–4) justices determined in *Olmstead* v. *United States* (1928). There was no actual entry, Chief Justice Taft wrote for the majority, only an enhanced sense of hearing. Nor could an overheard conversation qualify as a seizure because the Fourth Amendment referred only to physical items.

This literal interpretation brought impassioned dissents. Justice Holmes condemned illegal wire tapping, calling it a "dirty business" and concluding "it a less evil that some criminal should escape than that the government should play an ignoble part." Brandeis too saw the issue in moral terms—"if the government becomes a lawbreaker, it breeds contempt for the law"—but he went beyond his colleague in arguing for a more expansive definition of the terms search and seizure. The framers of the Constitution, he wrote, "conferred, as against the Government, the right to be let alone—the most comprehensive of rights, and the right most valued by civilized man.'' These themes were for the future. Although Congress in 1934 prohibited the use of wire-tap evidence in federal courts, not until 1967 did the Court decide that the Fourth Amendment protects people, not places, and bring wire tapping under the reach of the Fourth Amendment.[24]

These exceptions were departures from the Court's liberal construction of Fourth Amendment guarantees. Still, the sweeping assertions of the amendment's protection applied only to federal courts. The justices' unswerving adherence to the concept of dual federalism, except for economic regulations, meant states retained exclusive authority to define rights of the accused in trials under state law. Jose Antonio Hurtado's appeal of his murder conviction in 1884 revealed just how firm was the justices' commitment to this principle. No one proclaimed Hurtado's innocence. By the undisputed testimony of numerous witnesses, he cold-bloodedly shot his wife's lover three times, once in the back, and then pistol-whipped the dying man. A police court determined that there was probable cause to hold Hurtado, and the district attorney several days later filed charges in the Sacramento, California, court. This procedure departed significantly from the indictment required in federal and most state courts, but it was permitted by the California Constitution of 1879. The issue on appeal before the U. S. Supreme Court was straightforward: did the due process clause of the Fourteenth Amendment incorporate guarantees of the federal Bill of Rights and make them binding on the states?[25]

Since the war the number of due process challenges to state policies had mushroomed, much to the consternation of the Court, which claimed in an 1878 case that ''there exists some strange misconception of the scope of this provision as found in the XIVth Amendment.''[26] In a series of cases the justices demonstrated a reluctance to apply any of the Bill of Rights to the states, especially in criminal matters. *Hurtado* provided the opportunity to discuss the question fully and address specifically the amendment's relationship, if any, to rights of the accused under state criminal process.

Writing for the majority, Justice Matthews rejected the argument that due process required indictment by a grand jury. The meaning of due process was the same in both the Fifth and Fourteenth Amendments, the justice concluded. Due process under the latter amendment did not include indictment because the former amendment listed indictment and due process as separate provisions. Under a rule of interpretation that required the court to assume no part of the Constitution was unnecessary or superfluous, Matthews argued that the framers at Philadelphia did not consider grand-jury indictment to be part of due process of law or they would not have noted it especially.

The decision did not rest on this interpretation alone. The concept of due process was flexible; it "was made for an undefined and expanding future," Matthews wrote. The Constitution did not impose traditional common-law procedures on the states but left them free to re-cast their criminal process, as nine states had chosen to do by modifying or abandoning grand jury indictments as the method of initiating prosecutions. The Court conceded that no state could interfere with "fundamental principles of liberty and justice," but states could determine what those principles were. Matthews cited with approval an earlier equal protection case involving civil procedure: "The Fourteenth Amendment does not profess to secure to all persons in the United States the benefit of the same laws and the same remedies. Great diversities may exist . . . in two States separated only by an imaginary line. On one side there might be a right of trial by jury, and on the other side no such right. Each state prescribes its own modes of judicial proceeding." There was, the Court's opinion implied, no difference between litigants in a civil proceeding and defendants in a criminal trial.[27]

One justice differed sharply with his colleagues. John Marshall Harlan, a tall, tobacco-chewing Kentuckian appointed to the Court in 1877, attacked the conclusion that states were free to experiment with due process. How, he asked, could the justices fail to consider grand jury indictment a fundamental principle of liberty and justice? Harlan especially challenged the assertion that the due process clauses of the Fifth and Fourteenth Amendments were the same, thus removing a right to a grand jury indictment because the Fifth Amendment listed indictment and due process separately. Logically, this meant that none of the Bill of Rights, including those of speech or press or the rights to counsel or bail, could be protected against state action under the Fourteenth Amendment. To Harlan, such a conclusion was contrary to experience—what else, after all, could the Civil War amendments mean?—and precluded the only position consistent with the nation's republican traditions, namely, total incorporation of the Bill of Rights in the due process clause of the

Fourteenth Amendment. The amendment's intent was clear: "to impose upon the States the same restrictions, in respect of proceedings involving life, liberty and property, which had been imposed upon the general government."[28]

Harlan remained a minority of one. In case after case, the Court resisted the idea that the Bill of Rights applied to state criminal process. Only when the issue involved rights of blacks, such as in the jury cases discussed earlier, did a majority of justices apply the amendment. Even then, the Court justified its action under the equal protection clause rather than the due process provision. On three occasions in the 1890s two colleagues joined the Kentucky jurist in dissent against the majority's refusal to apply the Eighth Amendment's ban on cruel and unusual punishments to the state, but in most instances Harlan was a lonely voice in calling for the nationalization of due process guarantees for the accused. The Court found ways to protect substantive property rights from state interference by invoking the Fourteenth Amendment's due process language, but it rejected national protection for the privilege against self-incrimination and even held that jury trial was not a secured right.[29]

The denial of a universal privilege against self-incrimination came in *Twining* v. *New Jersey* (1908), a benchmark case in the development of the modern Bill of Rights. Twining was president of a New Jersey trust company who, in a tawdry scheme, sold his shares in a failing bank to his own company, thus salvaging his personal investment and saddling the trust company with the responsibility for the bank's losses. Prosecuted on a variety of criminal charges, Twining was finally convicted, in part because the judge had drawn a negative inference from the defendant's refusal to testify in his own behalf. New Jersey law allowed this conclusion, even though other state and federal courts adopted strict rules to guard against such a result.

Common-law procedures did not permit defendants to testify, in the belief that a strong instinct for self-protection would make such testimony untrustworthy. Most states and the federal government adopted statutes in the 1870s making defendants competent witnesses in criminal trials, with the stipulation that refusal to testify did not imply guilt. Yet the U. S. Supreme Court upheld Twining's conviction after concluding that the right against self-incrimination, while universally accepted in American law, was "not an essential part of due process, but . . . a wise and beneficent rule of evidence." Neither the Fifth Amendment's express language concerning self-incrimination nor its guarantee of due process secured the privilege from state action.[30]

If the matter had ended there, then the case would have simply been one of a long series in which the Court denied Bill of Rights' protection to criminal defendants in state courts. But the majority opinion conceded the due process clause of the Fourteenth Amendment might safeguard rights similar to those in the Bill of Rights, not because the first eight amendments applied to the states but "because they are of such a nature that they are included in the conception of due process of law." The Bill of Rights still abridged federal power only, although now, the Court suggested, the Fourteenth Amendment might impose due process requirements on the states that were similar, but not identical, to rights protected by the Constitution. It was a cautious and unsatisfying decision, reflecting the age's uncertain and changing assumptions about the nature of federalism and responsibility for criminal process. Still, it offered the promise that future decisions would extend Bill of Rights' protections by incorporating them into a definition of due process.[31]

Twining v. *New Jersey* signaled the way for the eventual nationalization of federal guarantees for the criminally accused. Yet change came slowly. The years following World War I were not hospitable to the expansion of civil liberties. A disillusioning war with its resulting economic dislocations and xenophobia, the Red Scare, a new prosperity, the emergence of organized crime, and the Progressive demise—all contributed to a climate that rejected any advance on the promise of the *Twining* decision. Not until the 1930s did the justices begin selectively incorporating rights under the amendment's due process clause. And never did the Court embrace Justice Harlan's call for total incorporation, even though his vision remained a powerful one for individuals who sought to extend the amendment's reach.

The Court's decisions during the late nineteenth and early twentieth centuries conformed to traditional interpretations of defendants' rights and reaffirmed the era's understanding of the line between federal and state authority. They also had little relevance to the practices and procedures of local law enforcement, including trial courts. There, the language of rights often seemed inapplicable to the requirements of order.

The criminal justice system—if, indeed, the jumble of courts and agencies, some with overlapping jurisdiction, could be termed a system at all—experienced significant change from 1870 to 1920. Complexity and specialization marked the process by the end of the century. Especially in the emerging cities, a web of specialized institutions replaced the relatively simple antebellum structure of justices of the peace and circuit courts. Police courts tried minor offenses, while separate criminal courts handled more serious matters. Juvenile courts received defendants under a certain age, usually 14 or 16. Probation officers and parole boards were also part of an increasingly complex legal system. Instead of operating as a well-integrated whole, these agencies often functioned independently, each constituting a separate layer of justice with its own procedures and customs for addressing problems of criminal conduct.[32]

Such specialization spurred the development of a law enforcement bureaucracy. Laymen and part-timers had dominated the pre-Civil War police and courts, but by the 1920s the criminal process embraced a substantial number of professional workers. Prosecutors and trial judges assumed their responsibilities full-time, policemen sought the status of a career, and probation officers became employees of the court.[33]

This burgeoning professionalism paralleled a shift in focus from the crime to the criminal. The antebellum emphasis on reformation found new expression in the postwar decades as theorists and practitioners of criminal justice sought clues in the criminal's background to discover whether cure was possible. Guiding this effort was the research of an Italian doctor, Cesare Lambrusco, who published detailed observations of criminals in several works, including his major book, *Crime: Causes and Remedies* (1899), an early but flawed scientific study. Lambrusco suggested that there was a specific "criminal type" who could be distinguished from noncriminals through a number of genetically determined physical and behavioral traits. As a result, prosecutors and judges began to require information about the defendant's personality, background, character, and habits in the hope that punishments could be tailored to produce reform. The need for such information stimulated the growth of the criminal justice bureaucracy and justified the increased expenditure of public funds for its support. It also led to the growing use of indeterminate sentences, or prison terms with only a fixed maximum confinement, under the assumption that prison officials and parole boards could best determine when good behavior had become permanent and the offender again trusted to re-enter society.[34]

One result of this growing bureaucratization was an emphasis on efficiency, especially in processing defendants through the system. This trend, consistent with the norms of an industrializing society, had a significant impact on the practical meaning of due process. Perhaps the most striking development was the widespread practice of plea bargaining, a pre-trial agreement between the prosecutor and the defendant to exchange a guilty plea for a lighter sentence. Such agreements were not unknown earlier in the century, but they were not common, at least not in such explicit form. Antebellum courts received a number of guilty pleas, but typically admissions of guilt were not the result of a deal between the state and the accused. Rather, they constituted an "implicit bargain," in which the defendant pleads guilty with the clear expectation, often implied by previous sentences, that the judge will treat him leniently in exchange.[35]

The advent of plea bargaining was not a response to mounting case pressure. Several studies of nineteenth-century crime reveal a decline in the number of prosecutions for serious offenses. Order was of paramount concern in the cities, and much effort went into the control of rowdy and threatening behavior. Policemen had regular beats, and on their patrols they constantly imposed the social discipline necessary for urban life. Perhaps such vigilance dampened criminal activity, but for whatever reason the shift to bargained sentences did not result from frantic efforts to cope with a rising tide of urban crime. It came from the new bureaucratization of criminal justice. The police undoubtedly found it more efficient to exchange a reduced charge for information about past or planned crimes, and prosecutors discovered that they could process cases more quickly if they struck pre-trial deals. Police discretion and prosecutorial bargains also kept decisions in the hands of professionals and away from unreliable juries drawn from an increasingly polyglot population.[36]

Two concurrent developments strengthened the role of criminal justice professionals and lessened the influence of juries. Bench trial for felony cases became acceptable practice in several jurisdictions, and state legislatures enacted statutes that restricted even further the jury's power to decide both law and facts in criminal matters. In a bench trial, the defendant waives his right to a jury trial and submits his case directly to the judge on a plea of not guilty. Not allowed under common-law procedures, three states had adopted the practice by statute before the turn of the century. Numerous other states moved to restrict the jury's prerogative by clearly restricting its role to a determination of facts only. The alleged inefficiency of the jury strongly influenced both developments, as did a growing conviction that defendants should be permitted to waive even those rights linked most directly to traditional concepts of justice.[37]

State appellate courts were uneasy with these changes, especially plea bargaining, and repeatedly remanded cases reached under such arrangements. The Tennessee Supreme Court reversed a conviction in 1865 in which the defendant pled guilty to two counts of gambling in exchange for dismissal of eight similar charges. A public trial, the justices declared, "cannot be defeated by any deceit or device whatever." Other courts agreed. "No sort of pressure can be permitted to bring the party to forego any right or advantage however slight," wrote the Michigan court in 1879. "The law will not suffer the least weight to be put in the scale against him." In 1908 the Florida court also expressed a wary attitude: "The plea should be entirely voluntary by one competent to know the consequences and should not be induced by fear, misapprehension, persuasion, promises, inadvertence, or ignorance." The opinions reflected several concerns: the practice represented a perversion of due process; it amounted to a sale of justice; the bargain could not be kept unless the court abdicated its proper role as a neutral forum; and secrecy made the agreement anti-democratic and a threat to liberty.[38]

These appellate decisions did not slow the rapid growth of plea bargaining. Trial judges continued to accept agreements between prosecutors and defendants, especially in cities. Many of the accused were indeed guilty, so a negotiated plea ensured punishment while saving the court time and money. Culpable defendants rarely objected because the bargain invariably led to a lesser sentence. Not every court allowed the practice, of course. Plea bargains were less common in rural states where neither case pressure nor the demand for order required them. Some prosecutors tried to avoid such barter, but these officials were in the minority. State surveys of criminal justice in the 1920s revealed a heavy dependence on the guilty plea in big-city courts. In Chicago, 85 percent of all felony convictions resulted from an admission of guilt. The percentages in other cities were almost as high or even higher: Detroit, 78; Denver, 76; St. Louis, 84; Minneapolis, 90; Pittsburgh, 74; Los Angeles, 81.[39]

The extent of plea bargaining stunned contemporary observers, perhaps because criminal courts composed a distinct subculture hidden even to appellate courts and more genteel lawyers. Critics attacked "the spirit of auction" that attended the process of justice, but their comments revealed a greater concern that criminals would go unpunished than with any threat to due process. The New York Appellate Division complained that plea bargaining allowed the defendant "to escape . . . with punishment all too inadequate for the crime committed," while Roscoe Pound, eminent dean of Harvard Law School, characterized the practice as "a license to violate the law." Only a few observers noted the challenge to the rights of the accused. "The necessity for making a good record . . . may very well result in prosecutors overlooking the rights, privileges and immunities of the poor, ignorant fellow who . . . is induced to confess crime and plead guilty through hope of reward or fear of extreme punishment," wrote a law dean. And the Wickersham Commission, a federal task force on crime and justice, recorded the complaint of foreign-born defendants that attorneys encouraged guilty pleas after discovering there was no money to pay legal fees.[40]

The emergence of plea bargaining dramatized the vast difference between due process as described in law books and appellate opinions and due process as practiced in courts. The gap has always been present in American law; in many ways, the local and discretionary nature of criminal justice makes it inevitable. The conduct of trials in colonial and post-Revolutionary courts—eight to ten trials each day, defendants securing lawyers at the courthouse door, the same jurors serving in one trial after another—suggests that due process rarely existed in pristine form. It was a powerful political idea, but its routine expression was imperfect. Still, there were occasions, especially at trials of high drama, in which the whole panoply of rights was on full display. These moments lent substance to the concept of due process and thus reinforced its place in the constitutional order.

Criminal justice in Alameda County (Oakland), California, subject of an extended scholarly study, illustrates the way in which local courts sidestepped the requirements of due process. At least three systems of justice operated in the county courts, each a separate layer different in form, function, and method. Celebrated cases constituted the top tier. These crimes—murder, arson, and political scandal, chief among them—grabbed public attention and focused attention on the nature of adversary justice at its best. Lawyers dominated proceedings, exploiting every technicality and claiming every right for the accused. These were the cases that shaped public understanding of the criminal justice, and they were the cases that went up on appeal and became the heart of textbook law. But they were also uncommon and expensive.[41]

Ordinary, serious crime made up the second layer of justice in Alameda County. Property crimes, later traffic felonies, were the most common cases. There was little drama here. Everything was a matter of routine. Fewer than half the cases went to trial; there were many guilty pleas, many dismissals; only one of seven defendants who went to trial gained acquittal, or only 2 percent of all defendants charged with felonies. But this figure does not mean that the system of justice grew more harsh. Most defendants received informal acquittals through decisions not to prosecute. Such filtering of cases lessened the need for judge and jury. The debating skills of a lawyer were less important than an ability to work the system for a client's benefit. Prosecutors received plaudits for processing defendants, and judges supervised the activity and placed an official imprimatur on it. The system at this level did not correspond closely to theory. On balance, it was much more concerned with administrative efficiency than formal legal process.[42]

Justice and police courts formed the bottom layer of criminal justice in Alameda County. The volume of business conducted by these courts was overwhelming; drunkenness, assault, fighting, gambling—these offenses crowded the docket. The main purpose of prosecution was discipline of the working classes. Police trawled the streets, hauling in large numbers of offenders. Some drunks and vagrants repeatedly attended court, but many accused faced a judge for the first time. Prosecutors dismissed cases routinely, and convicted offenders received small fines and perhaps a night or two in jail. The object of all this activity was order, not punishment. Due process was not a primary concern of these petty courts: there were few attorneys, juries were rare, and defendants paraded through court in assembly-line fashion. The requirements of discipline and order, not rights, guided the behavior of police, prosecutors, and judges.[43]

Due process was not a dead letter in this California jurisdiction; neither did it govern the administration of justice. Concern for the rights of defendants appeared most clearly in the trials that engaged public attention. Crime control occupied center stage in less visible cases. Here the process of justice was more murky, with much bargaining and less adherence to legal form. But emphasis on administrative efficiency should not imply an absence of protection for the accused. Judges and lawyers absorbed the ideals of due process in their training and practiced them whenever possible. It was simply that other circumstances—for instance, the public demand for order or a defendant's scarce financial resources—limited the opportunities for such ideals to triumph uncontested.

The Alameda County judicial system neither exalted nor ignored due process. Instead, it reflected the norms of the general society. It did what it was supposed to do—punish criminals—and it reminded everyone of the overarching values of the constitutional order. Not every jurisdiction could make that claim. In some areas of the nation, and certainly for some defendants, there was no due process and the claims of law went unacknowledged.

First-generation immigrants always had found courts to be unresponsive, if not antagonistic, and had discovered that protections accorded to other citizens did not apply to them in equal measure. Late nineteenth-century arrivals from Eastern Europe and Asia learned what Germans and Irish settlers had experienced decades earlier—due process was, in its fullest expression, an Anglo-Saxon privilege.[44] This lesson also applied with brutal force to blacks, especially in the South, who witnessed firsthand all the law's rigors but little of its majesty.

It is difficult for modern observers to comprehend the almost total denial of due process to thousands of black defendants during these years. But the record is unmistakable. When blacks killed, raped, or robbed blacks, white officials often treated the offense casually, sometimes prosecuting and sometimes ignoring the crime, depending on the status of defendant or victim and his relationship to whites. Such intraracial crime did not command white attention. "We have very little crime," a Mississippian bragged in the 1930s. "Of course, Negroes knife each other occasionally, but there is little *real* crime." When blacks stood trial for offenses against other blacks, they were far more likely than white defendants to be offered a plea bargain, to lack effective counsel, and to have the judge or prosecutor rush the proceedings. Separate standards— "Negro law" in commmon parlance—denied blacks the protections of due process because it served white interests. It produced "perfectly satisfactory results," a trial judge explained: defendants escaped the hangman, taxpayers avoided the expense of lengthy trials, and the prison farm got additional field hands.[45]

Interracial crime was a far different story. Nearly any decent white man could escape punishment for killing a black, whatever the circumstances. Except for particularly heinous or shocking crimes, district attorneys would not prosecute, white lawyers were reluctant to accept such cases, and white juries would not convict. If they were fortunate, black defendants stood trial, although the proceedings were often a mere parody of justice. Tainted evidence, irrelevant testimony, outrageous prosecutorial antics, and prejudicial jury instructions deprived due process of all substantive meaning. Usually counsel was available, but defense attorneys, almost always white, rarely pursued issues or points of law to the defendant's advantage because of fear of losing clients. To be sure, there were fair judges and conscientious attorneys, but these men were few compared to the many who surrendered the ideals of equal justice to the demands of white supremacy.[46]

The rush to judgment was extreme for black on white crimes, even in courtrooms where judges normally pushed cases to rapid conclusion. Indictment, trial, and conviction could occur in a matter of days, especially when community passions were inflamed. At times, one observer noted, "it is somewhat difficult to draw . . . a sharp line marking off distinctly the point where the lynching spirit stops and the spirit of legal procedure begins." One Mississippi circuit judge, hoping to avert mob action in 1908, even negotiated a sentence for a black defendant before the prosecutor filed charges. Such travesty of justice was routine, although few officials went so far as to pronounce sentence before trial began. Most black defendants recognized that protest was futile. Too often the alternative to a courtroom charade was vengeful punishment meted out by a mob bent on preserving white honor or power.[47]

For blacks who received a safe trial, there was no practical route of appeal. Judicial review was not a realistic alternative for social mudsills, especially Negroes. Appeals were costly and required the continued assistance of court-appointed attorneys, most of whom lost interest upon hearing the verdict. Even when available, appellate review did not guarantee justice. State supreme courts charted an uneven course in these cases. Insulated from pressures of the moment, the high bench sometimes reversed convictions and chastised judges and lawyers who departed from color-blind standards. Just as often, the justices overlooked obvious errors and pursued technicalities that permitted convictions to stand. Unlike antebellum judges who corrected injustice in individual cases without undermining the institution of slavery, the late nineteenth-century southern bench could never ignore the claims of white supremacy or irrational fears of black violence.[48]

There is a certain irony in the development of due process in the late nineteenth and early twentieth centuries. From the highest courts came formal support for the rights of the accused. There was no retreat from earlier beliefs that such guarantees were necessary for true liberty to exist. But this exaltation of rights bore slight correspondence to the practice of criminal justice. In trial courts and on police beats the emphasis was on administrative efficiency. There was no plan to subvert constitutional protections. These rights simply appeared irrelevant to the more pressing task of processing defendants through the system. Most citizens undoubtedly believed that they enjoyed the full protection of the law, and perhaps they were right—if they were white and middle-class.

Gradually the cracks in the foundation of rights became too obvious to ignore. Studies of criminal justice in the 1920s exposed the inner workings of courts and police and stimulated a public clamor for reform. The demand for social justice, so much a part of the first decades of the twentieth century, directed attention to those areas in which the reality of American life did not fit democratic ideals. Finally, the emergence of professional groups created a demand for universal standards that frequently clashed with local values and prejudices. The time was ripe for change, and beginning in the 1930s a generation of judges and lawmakers would devote considerable effort to redefining due process. In doing so, they extended the promise of the Revolution of 1776. But in the quest for universal norms, they also unleashed a powerful debate on the terms of justice for the accused.

5

FAIR TRIAL, FEDERALISM, AND RIGHTS OF THE ACCUSED

Few criminal cases lead to claims of injustice. Defendants usually accept the plea bargain offered to them or, upon trial, do not challenge the jury's verdict. There is rarely any public scrutiny of criminal courts because most proceedings are routine. But some trials are so obviously unjust that they command attention and compel a reexamination of the practice of criminal justice. The prosecution of the Scottsboro boys in 1931 was such an incident, and it signaled the beginning of a judicial trend to extend the protection of the federal Bill of Rights to state criminal defendants.

On March 25, 1931, a group of hoboes complained to a deputy sheriff near Scottsboro, Alabama, that a "bunch of Negroes" on a Memphis-bound freight train had attacked them. The claim was a serious one in the oppressive racial environment of the Deep South. It became explosive when a hastily gathered posse discovered two white girls dressed in men's clothing in the same railroad car as nine black youths. The teenaged girls, recognizing their serious breach of Jim Crow laws, alleged that the boys, ranging in age from 13 to 19, had repeatedly raped them. Word of the incident spread rapidly around the rural county. By the time the youths reached the Scottsboro jail only the judge's promise of speedy punishment kept an angry mob from resorting to lynch law.[1]

The trial was a legal sham. Aware that state law required counsel for anyone charged with a capital crime, the judge appointed all seven members of the Scottsboro bar as defense attorneys. One by one, the lawyers withdrew from the case. Left to defend the accused was an unreliable seventy-year-old lawyer. Aiding the defense was an alcoholic white attorney from Chattanooga, hired by a group of concerned black ministers because he had on occasion taken cases for Negroes. The trial—actually four separate cases—proceeded swiftly: four days after court opened eight of the accused stood before the judge to receive the death sentence. The verdict was no surprise, yet it was immensely satisfying to the three thousand people who crowded the small town to witness the trial, a throng considered so volatile that the state National Guard mounted machine guns on the courthouse steps to control it.[2]

The case was not over, however. Widespread newspaper coverage and the novelty of eight men sentenced to death for the same crime on the same day had attracted the attention of important national groups, especially the National Association for the Advancement of Colored People and the Communist Party of the United States. Pursuing different agendas, both organizations saw the trial as an opportunity to challenge the existing order. To the NAACP, the problem was a legal system that failed to grant black citizens a fair trial; to the Communist Party, a capitalist government had used law to trample an underclass. Each group wanted to represent the defendants on appeal, and each used the case to enlist public support for its larger efforts. In the process, the case became the cause célèbre of the decade.

In 1932 the Supreme Court ruled on the Scottsboro case, formally known as *Powell* v. *Alabama,* with conservative Justice George Sutherland speaking for the 7–2 majority. Attorneys for the appellants had asked the Court to apply the Bill of Rights to the states by incorporating its protection for defendants into the Fourteenth Amendment's guarantee of due process in all federal and state trials. Specifically, they sought reversal of the verdict on three grounds: lack of a fair trial, inadequacy of counsel, and exclusion of Negroes from Alabama juries.

The Court focused attention only on the issue of counsel, which Sutherland characterized as unacceptably casual. But what constitutional provision was at issue? Not the Sixth Amendment's right to counsel; it bound the federal courts alone. Sutherland found an answer in the due process language of the Fourteenth Amendment, despite the Court's earlier denial in *Hurtado* v. *California* (1884) that the phrase included any of the Bill of Rights. The logic was simple. State and federal precedents made the right to counsel central to the meaning of due process. By accepted definition, any action to deny this right would also deny due process. Thus, the Fourteenth Amendment embraced this guarantee, one similar but not necessarily identical to the provision for counsel in the Sixth Amendment, and extended its protection to capital defendants in state courts.[3]

Powell v. *Alabama* was a striking departure for the Court. In earlier cases, the justices had incorporated the rights of speech and press under Fourteenth Amendment protection because the justices deemed them fundamental to liberty, a problematic concept that, like due process, the framers in 1868 had failed to define. But always the Court refused to apply the criminal procedures required by the Bill of Rights to the states. Under *Powell,* the assistance of counsel, at least in capital cases, was now as worthy of constitutional protection as the right of speech. The jurisdictional wall separating state and federal power was beginning to crumble.

From the 1930s through the 1950s the Supreme Court grappled with the question of which rights were included in the Fourteenth Amendment phrase, due process of law. The catalog of nationalized rights— provisions of the Bill of Rights binding on the states—was quite extensive by the end of the three decades, especially given the previous absence of such guarantees, although the list pales when compared to current practice. Fundamental rights included limited protection against illegal searches and seizures (Fourth Amendment), coerced confessions (Fifth), public trial, impartial jury, and counsel (Sixth), and cruel and unusual punishments (Eighth). Other rights considered central by later Courts were not included: double jeopardy, protection against self-incrimination, and jury trial, among others.

The nationalization of the Bill of Rights travelled an uncertain course because the justices lacked a sure theoretical foundation for their decisions. There was no consensus on principles to guide interpretation of the amendments, in part because of the novelty of the idea that defendants' rights needed protection against state misconduct. Few judges doubted that injustice could—and did—occur in state criminal trials, but even many enlightened jurists accepted the traditional argument that classical federalism, with its curb of central power, offered the best security for individual liberty. Well into the twentieth century, commentators asserted the states' exclusive authority in criminal matters and the primacy of state constitutions in guaranteeing rights of the accused. Courts generally accepted this theory of federalism, and judges shouldered an obligation to maintain its careful distinctions.

The first decades of the new century witnessed a sweeping reassessment of these governmental roles, including the responsibility of the central government in areas previously reserved to states. Sparking this change was a new style of legal reasoning, sociological jurisprudence, which took its charge from Oliver Wendell Holmes' influential treatise, *The Common Law* (1881). "The life of the law has not been logic," Holmes wrote, "it has been experience." Law was always a product of its time and place; it reflected customs and embraced existing social and economic norms. It was not, as traditionalists maintained, a set of eternal principles from which objective judges could discover equally timeless and value-free rules. Benjamin Cardozo, legal scholar and later Supreme Court justice, and Roscoe Pound, then dean of the Harvard Law School, carried this message to a wider public audience and gained acceptance of the argument that law must be judged by results, not by the application of formal reasoning.[4]

Constitutional scholars most often associate the triumph of sociological jurisprudence with federal regulation of the economy during and after the Great Depression. Less well recognized is its impact on nationalization of rights of the accused. The post-World War I years produced startling examples of the failure of state governments to protect even the most basic rights of criminal defendants. Especially vulnerable were defendants from ethnic or other minority groups. The Red Scare of 1919 was only the first episode in a long series of events that revealed the xenophobia present in American society. Fueled by a belief that Bolsheviks were the cause of most social unrest and labor strife, federal and state agencies arrested and deported members of socialist groups, seized and burned records of radical organizations, and harassed and arrested numerous other citizens identified with left-wing activities.[5]

This wholesale violation of civil liberties had its origin in hatred directed against foreigners and so-called hyphenated Americans, particularly German-Americans, many of whom had opposed United States' involvement in World War I. Dissent became a popular synonym for disloyalty. Governments at all levels passed sedition and criminal syndicalism laws to punish advocacy of and association with policies, organizations, and activities deemed un-American. This climate of political repression fostered nativist attacks on individuals whose only "crime" was their ethnic or religious heritage. Catholics and Jews were frequent suspects. Local vigilante groups and national organizations alike used fear, exclusion, and illegal tactics to threaten alleged subversives and undesirables, often with the cooperation of local, state, and federal authorities. The revived Ku Klux Klan, for example, so dominated midwestern politics in the early 1920s that many office-seekers believed membership to be an unwritten requirement for election.[6]

The immediate postwar years witnessed other events that demonstrated the insecurity of defendants' rights under state protection. During the long, hot summer of 1919, at least twenty major racial disturbances erupted in the nation's cities, most of them in the North. The Chicago riot was the single worst episode, with thirty-eight dead and hundreds injured after a week of lawlessness. Special commissions investigated the riots and found a general pattern of white aggression and black retaliation. These reports also revealed serious police misconduct. Not only had policemen engaged in discriminatory law enforcement before and during the riots, they often were rioters themselves.[7] The racial conflict in northern cities had an uglier counterpart in the rural South where lynching became a routine white response to serious black misbehavior: angry mobs accounted for no fewer than 3,383 black deaths from 1882–1936.[8]

Official disregard for individual rights was not limited to episodes of racial or ethnic conflict. It was endemic in American law enforcement, as a major national investigation revealed in 1931. President Herbert Hoover appointed the National Commission on Law Observance and Enforcement in 1929 at the height of public concern over the gangland crime and criminal disorder associated with prohibition. The Wickersham Commission, known after its chairman, former Attorney General George Wickersham, issued fourteen volumes, but only one, Report 11: *Lawlessness in Law Enforcement,* attracted much attention. Page after page documented the regular practice of physical brutality, the so-called "third degree," by police departments across the country. Such tactics showed a striking contempt, sometimes expressed openly, for rights guaranteed by state and federal constitutions.[9]

The abuse of individual rights angered many Americans, some of whom organized to defend victims of governmental lawlessness. Prominent among the groups dedicated to protecting constitutional rights was the American Civil Liberties Union, originally established during the war to represent conscientious objectors who refused military service. The emergence of the ACLU signaled the potential of significant change in the administration of criminal justice. Never before had there been a national group that championed the rights of individuals against official and private abuses. Its creation reflected the victory of sociological jurisprudence over older, more formal ways of thinking about constitutional guarantees.[10]

At first the ACLU sought primarily to deny state interference with First Amendment freedoms; and in several important decisions in the 1920s, the Supreme Court agreed that the Fourteenth Amendment protected these rights against infringement by states. Emboldened by the success of its strategy, the ACLU gradually turned attention to miscarriages of criminal justice. Soon other organizations, notably the NAACP and International Labor Defense, adopted similar tactics. By the 1930s numerous national groups were ready to lend legal assistance and financial help in an effort to nationalize the Bill of Rights for criminal defendants.

Even so, and despite the promise of the *Scottsboro* decision, the Supreme Court resisted attempts to incorporate the protection of the Fourth, Fifth, and Sixth Amendments into a national standard. In 1936, for example, in *Brown* v. *Mississippi*, the justices overturned the conviction of three Negroes who had confessed to capital murder only after having been severely beaten and subjected to other physical abuse. A unanimous Court held that the state's use of coerced confessions denied the defendants a fair trial. Extorting a confession by torture was ''revolting to the sense of justice'' and violated a principle ''so rooted in the traditions and conscience of our people as to be ranked fundamental.'' But it did not transgress the Fifth Amendment's protection against self-incrimination. A state was free to establish whatever criminal procedures fit its own conception of public policy. It could even abandon practices required by the U. S. Constitution. The only restrictions imposed by the Fourteenth Amendment were those elements fundamental to justice. ''Because a state may dispense with a jury trial,'' Chief Justice Hughes wrote, ''it does not follow that it may substitute trial by ordeal. The rack and torture chamber may not be substituted for the witness chair.''[11]

The *Brown* decision suggested the Court had reached a consensus on a guide through the thicket of claims made by defendants who sought national protection of their rights. Procedures fundamental to a fair trial were central to the Fourteenth Amendment's conception of due process; other practices were beyond its scope. The next year, 1937, the landmark case *Palko* v. *Connecticut* confirmed this distinction. A Connecticut jury had found a petty thief, Frank Palko, guilty of the second-degree murder of two Bridgeport policemen. The prosecution appealed to the Supreme Court of Errors under a law that granted a new trial if errors prejudicial to the state had occurred. A second trial resulted in a death sentence for first-degree murder. On appeal, Palko's court-appointed attorney objected that the re-trial constituted double jeopardy in violation of state and federal constitutions. Although the statute reversed common-law procedure, the state supreme court found no error and allowed the conviction to stand.

The U. S. Supreme Court agreed. In one of the most influential opinions issued from the high bench, Justice Benjamin Cardozo rejected the argument that the Bill of Rights applied to states through the Fourteenth Amendment. The *Hurtado* precedent restricted the guarantee of grand jury indictment to the federal government alone; the Fifth Amendment protection against self-incrimination "will fail if the state elects to end it." Also, trial by jury could be modified or abolished by states without constitutional protest. Yet, Cardozo conceded, the Court had found certain rights—speech, press, and right to counsel—applicable in every state. What distinguished national rights protected by the Fourteenth Amendment from privileges subject to state control? The answer was seductively simple: the right in question must be essential to "a scheme of ordered liberty."[12]

Cardozo's artful phrase captured the sentiment of the Court—only one justice dissented—but it set an uncertain standard for future decisions. The opinion defined its key principle by reference to equally vague language. Rights received constitutional protection if their denial imposed "hardships so shocking that our polity will not endure it" or if the actions of government violated the "fundamental principles of liberty and justice which lie at the base of all our civil and political institutions." Much more clearly expressed was Cardozo's belief that a free society depended upon freedom of speech and expression. These core rights formed "the indispensable condition for nearly every other form of freedom."[13]

Rights of the accused existed on a different scale of values. Here, only the guarantee of a fair trial was central to liberty. The several states could employ widely different criminal procedures without violating a claim to fair treatment. Neither protection from self-incrimination or a grand jury indictment was fundamental to a fair trial, nor was the right against double jeopardy or even to a trial by jury. But the assistance of counsel was an integral part of federally guaranteed due process, if circumstances revealed it was "essential to the substance of a hearing."[14]

The fair trial test meant that the Court would decide case by case which rights of the accused enjoyed constitutional protection. It suggested that the values and attitudes of individual judges would determine which state procedures created such hardships or so shocked the conscience that they denied fair treatment. Yet the test also provided a method for modernizing the Bill of Rights by inviting justices to extend liberties if modern conditions required it.

Some members of the Court accepted such judicial discretion as inescapable, but other justices distrusted any approach that allowed judges to substitute their personal notions of fairness for an objective standard. Chief among those who sought more definitive criteria was Associate Justice Hugo Black, a long-time Democratic politician from Alabama and a staunch Senate supporter of President Franklin Roosevelt's reform policies. Black thought the fair trial test of defendants' rights too reminiscent of an earlier Court's attempt to make the due process clause the bulwark of its conservative economic philosophy. More defensible, he argued, was an acknowledgment that the framers of the Fourteenth Amendment intended to incorporate the Bill of Rights into the due process clause and to apply these rights as limits upon state action. This position, often called the total incorporation theory, had considerable appeal. It was easy to express, simple to apply, and embraced a conviction that individual rights should not vary from state to state.[15]

Total incorporation also promised to remove the Court from a doctrinal nightmare, namely, its recurrent assertion, first announced in *Hurtado* v. *California,* that the Bill of Rights and Fourteenth Amendment carried different meanings even when the same right was at issue. Under the fair trial test, the justices frequently found themselves deciding that a right essential to fair proceedings under the Fourteenth Amendment's due process clause—assistance of counsel, for instance—was not identical to the right guaranteed in federal trials by the Sixth Amendment. It was only a similar right. Otherwise, the framers of the Fourteenth Amendment would have repeated needlessly a right already granted. The doctrine of nonsuperfluousness, or the assumption that the Constitution was not internally redundant, had trapped the Court in an arcane debate that not even scholars understood completely. Total incorporation would allow the Court to escape the dilemma. It also would change radically the nature of the federal system; and it was on these grounds that the Court engaged in a debate that shaped the rights of defendants for the next few decades.[16]

The argument for total incorporation was unpersuasive to Felix Frankfurther, a long-time Harvard law professor who came to the Court after membership in the New Deal's famed "brain trust." Appointed in 1939 to the seat previously held both by Holmes and Cardozo, Frankfurter was heir to his predecessors' judicial philosophy. The Fourteenth Amendment's due process clause, he maintained, did not require a close reading of case records to determine if the prosecution violated any protection accorded by the first eight amendments. Rather, the clause called for "an exercise of judgment upon the whole course of the proceedings" to determine "whether they offend those canons of decency and fairness which express the notions of justice of English-speaking peoples."[17]

Like Holmes and Cardozo, Frankfurter believed that due process incorporated fundamental values, one of which was fairness, and that judges could dispassionately discover and apply these values to claims of injustice. He also recognized that attaching the Bill of Rights to the states through the Fourteenth Amendment's due process clause would alter irrevocably the federal division of governmental power, a fundamental principle of American constitutionalsim. Popular government demanded judicial deference to the judgment of elected representatives. Even in the area of civil liberties, legislative actions should be respected unless they flagrantly defied the community's sense of values.[18]

Procedural rights needed closer scrutiny, Frankfurter argued, because "the history of liberty has largely been the history of observance of procedural safeguards."[19] But here, too, the Court could only require that states enforce fundamental principles of liberty and justice. Review of criminal process, long the sole prerogative of the states, was a delicate matter. The Supreme Court should intervene only when states denied or refused to enforce appropriate constitutional guarantees. Due process, after all, was not solely a federal standard. It was a concept that expressed local values arising from different historical and practical considerations.

These divergent circumstances should be recognized insofar as they did not conflict with traditionally accepted Anglo-Saxon principles of justice.

The dispute between Black and Frankfurter was symptomatic of the Court's deep divisions in the 1940s and 1950s concerning nationalization of the Bill of Rights for criminal defendants. No one denied the importance of guaranteeing fair procedures. If anything, the rise of European and Asian police-states intensified the Court's sense of responsibility for careful evaluation of the administration of justice. But beyond a general concern for fairness in state trials, the justices could not agree on what their role should be.

Early in the decade the Court appeared to be moving toward a more expansive interpretation of defendants' rights. An opinion in a coerced-confession case, *Chambers* v. *Florida* (1940), clearly acknowledged that the federal government had a duty to guarantee fair trials in state as well as federal courts. The due process clause of the Fourteenth Amendment, Black wrote for the majority, "was intended to guarantee procedural standards adequate and appropriate, then and thereafter, to protect, at all times, people charged with or suspected of crime by those holding positions of power and authority."[20]

The problem, as always, was the definition of fair trial. Coerced confessions were unfair, but what other procedural guarantees of the Bill of Rights were essential to due process? Legal commentators had long regarded jury trial as a bulwark of Anglo-American justice, but when faced with the question of whether the Sixth Amendment required it for state trials the Court could not reach agreement. In several cases from 1942 to 1948, the justices first extended the limitation to state courts, only to return to an earlier position that permitted wide diversity of practice. Search and seizure cases received more consistent treatment, with the Court upholding governmental subterfuge and wiretaps to gain incriminating evidence. But in almost every case the justices found themselves deeply divided.

Even the requirement of counsel in all criminal trials could not gather a consensus, despite the *Scottsboro* ruling that it was necessary in capital cases. Until the 1930s judicial opinion agreed that the Sixth Amendment had simply ended the common-law practice prohibiting counsel in felony cases other than treason. Federal and state courts had no constitutional obligation to appoint counsel for indigent defendants. (The *Scottsboro* decision invoked the fair trial interpretation of due process, not the Sixth Amendment.) By 1938, the Court appeared ready to draw a different conclusion. When confronted with the case of two nearly illiterate Marines who were tried, convicted, and sentenced in federal court without legal representation, the justices held that "the Sixth Amendment withholds from federal courts, in all criminal proceedings, the power and authority to deprive an accused of his life or liberty unless he waives or has assistance of counsel." The new rule rested on the "realistic recognition . . . that the average defendant does not have the professional legal skill to protect himself . . . , wherein the prosecution is presented by experienced and learned counsel."[21]

Yet four years later, in *Betts* v. *Brady* (1942), the Court expressed serious doubt that the right to counsel was in every circumstance fundamental to a fair trial. The case came from Maryland, where an indigent defendant charged with robbery had been denied court-appointed counsel because it was not county practice except in prosecutions for murder or rape. Justice Roberts, for the 6–3 majority, denied that the Fourteenth Amendment's due process clause obligated the states to provide counsel. The right was not "dictated by natural, inherent and fundamental principles of fairness." It was a matter of legislative policy, and here the record was plain: "in the great majority of the States, it has been the considered judgment of the people, their representatives and their courts that appointment of counsel is not a fundamental right, essential to a fair trial."[22]

The *Betts* decision reaffirmed the Court's traditional interpretation of due process, even as it sharply limited the effect of the *Scottsboro* case. A high esteem for local practice as a necessary element of federalism outweighed the attractive simplicity of sweeping national rights. Due process, as Justice Frankfurter asserted in a later case, "is not to be turned into a destructive dogma. . . . It does not militate against respect for the deeply rooted systems of criminal justice in the States."[23] This stance meant the Court would continue to measure state criminal procedures case by case against its own criteria of fairness, judging the total circumstances rather than specific denials of rights. Each case depended on its own facts.

Not every justice agreed. A minority pressed for extending the Fourteenth Amendment's reach to all jurisdictions, federal and state. Justice Douglas succinctly captured the opposition logic in a later rejoinder to Frankfurter's position: "I fail to see why it is due process to deny an accused the benefit of counsel in a state court when by constitutional standards the benefit could not be withheld from him in a federal court."[24] But in general the Court shied from advancing a more universal rule. The practice of criminal justice was indeed local; and the high bench stood primarily as a court of last resort to ensure fairness.

At times the lack of federal oversight appeared to sanction injustice. In a notorious case of police brutality, a Georgia sheriff had beaten a black prisoner to death. When state authorities refused to prosecute, the U. S. Department of Justice sought to use Reconstruction-era civil rights acts to force a trial under federal law. The Court split acrimoniously. The statutes were admittedly vague, failing to provide clear standards of guilt, but the crime was a heinous one. The deeply divided justices ordered a new trial, with the minority—led by Frankfurter—voicing its alarm that this action portended massive federal interference into state criminal procedure. The solution for a breakdown in local justice, Frankfurter argued in dissent, was to encourage the people through their state legislatures to correct abuses with new statutes. Such faith in the democratic process could hardly have comforted blacks who already existed at the margins of southern society and had no effective voice in government.[25]

In 1947 the Court settled, at least temporarily, the issue that had dogged its interpretation of the Fourteenth Amendment since Cardozo's landmark opinion in *Palko* v. *Connecticut* ten years earlier. Under review was the capital conviction of Admiral Dewey Adamson, a sixty-four-year-old black man from Los Angeles, whose refusal to testify at trial allowed the prosecutor under state law to draw an inference of guilt. The legal issue was self-incrimination; the constitutional question was whether the Fifth Amendment protection applied to California through the Fourteenth Amendment; but the Court debate centered on the concept of total incorporation.

Four justices, led by Black, supported the argument that the Amendment's due process clause embraced the first eight amendments, thus limiting state actions. Never before or since had total incorporation gained such support on the Court. Still, a majority of justices rejected the argument in favor of the standard first advanced by Holmes and confirmed by Cardozo. Justice Frankfurter was the apparent victor in what had become a continuing legal skirmish. Fundamental fairness, captured in the notion of fair trial, remained the Court's lodestone in deciphering the meaning of due process.[26]

The decision in *Adamson* v. *California* represented a Pyrrhic triumph for the advocates of a fair trial interpretation of the Fourteenth Amendment's due process clause. It slowed but did not block the Court's scrutiny of state criminal process. Finally, in the due process revolution of the 1960s, it disappeared as a guiding interpretive principle, replaced in turn by selective incorporation, a standard that with few exceptions completed the nationalization of the Bill of Rights.

Notwithstanding its expressed reluctance to interfere with state procedures, the Court's adherence to the fair trial test led to small gains in creating national standards of due process. For example, the justices reversed a decision from the Michigan Supreme Court that upheld the state's use of a one-man grand jury as an investigative weapon against criminal conspiracies. A 1917 Michigan law allowed circuit judges to constitute themselves as single-member grand juries, subpoena witnesses and examine them in secret, issue indictments, and sentence for contempt. The one-man grand jury, in other words, combined the powers of judge, inquisitor, and prosecutor in a single person, properly only a judge. Opponents of the procedure claimed it violated due process, but the state legislature refused to abandon the law and the state supreme court declared it constitutional.

The U. S. Supreme Court determined otherwise. Public trials were part of the nation's common-law heritage, as was the opportunity for persons to defend themselves. Michigan's one-man grand jury violated these principles. Even though Justice Black wrote the opinion, the Court reached its decision by applying the fair trial test, not by incorporating the public trial guarantee of the Sixth Amendment in the Fourteenth Amendment's due process clause. The effect was the same: states did not have unlimited discretion to experiment with criminal procedures.[27]

More important in the nationalization of the Bill of Rights was *Wolf* v. *Colorado* (1949), a case that raised questions about the Fourth Amendment's application to the states and its enforceability in state courts. At issue was the conviction of a Denver abortionist based on evidence seized after a warrantless search of his offices. In federal courts the exclusionary rule, adopted by the Supreme Court in *Weeks* v. *United States* (1914), would have prevented use of any illegally obtained evidence at trial. Under Colorado law the only test of admissibility was whether evidence was relevant and material. The question upon appeal was straightforward: did the Fourth Amendment's prohibition of unreasonable searches and seizures extend to states?

The Supreme Court affirmed Wolf's conviction. The due process clause, wrote Justice Frankfurter, did not incorporate the Bill of Rights. But "security of one's privacy against arbitrary intrusion by the police—which is at the core of the Fourth Amendment—is basic to a free society."[28] Under the fair trial test it was implicit in the scheme of ordered liberty and enforceable against states. The protection from warrantless searches included in the concept of due process was similar to, not identical with, the guarantee of the Fourth Amendment. The distinction was a scholarly one. The core of the Fourth Amendment, like the right to counsel in capital cases, applied to states through the Fourteenth Amendment.

Still, the decision did not help Wolf. His conviction stood because the exclusionary rule, the majority opinion concluded, was a judicially created guide that Congress could repeal. It was not a command of the Fourth Amendment and governed only federal trials. States could reject the principle—and indeed the vast majority of states allowed illegally seized evidence in criminal trials—without violating the Bill of Rights.[29]

Wolf v. *California* protected a right but denied a remedy. Even though the Fourth Amendment was a shield against warrantless searches and seizures, defendants in state courts could not bar evidence gained illegally. Traditional alternatives to the exclusionary rule—civil suits for damages or criminal prosecution of violating officers—were rarely successful, and most police departments and prosecutors were unwilling or unable to stop the practice. The illusory promise of the decision did not go unnoticed. "The Court," one justice wrote in a stinging dissent, "now allows what is indeed shabby business: lawlessness by officers of the law." Another justice concurred: the "version of the Fourth Amendment today held applicable to the States . . . is a pale and frayed carbon copy of the original."[30]

During the 1950s the Court's continued reliance on the fair trial test led to much confusion regarding which criminal procedures were acceptable. Some state practices it permitted, others it rejected, but no clear standard emerged to guide the actions of local law enforcement. Nowhere were problems more apparent than in the justices' attempt to fix more precisely the meaning of due process and its application to the states. In 1952 the

Court modified the *Wolf* decision to exclude from state trials any illegal evidence gained by violent means. The facts in *Rochin* v. *California*—forcible extraction of narcotic capsules from the defendant's stomach—shocked the justices. Therein lay the rationale for the decision. The actions of law officers were "bound to offend even hardened sensibilities. . . . To sanction the brutal conduct . . . would be to afford brutality the cloak of law."[31] The Court's sense of justice precluded such approval.

Yet over the next five years two similar instances of official misconduct produced dramatically different results. In 1954, the Court considered whether a nonviolent search might be so repugnant it required exclusion of seized evidence. The case involved repeated unauthorized police entries into the home of an alleged bookmaker to hide microphones and monitor conversations. The justices once again registered their concern: "Few police measures have come to our attention that more flagrantly, deliberately, and persistently violated" a citizen's rights. But a 5–4 majority sustained the conviction, although with five separate opinions. The lack of bodily contact was crucial. There was no physical coercion, so the evidence was admissible.[32] Even this point was obscured three years later when the Court upheld a conviction for involuntary manslaughter while intoxicated based upon a blood sample drawn without consent from the unconscious defendant.[33]

The Court's decisions had produced only the most nebulous standards to guide law officers. Increasingly, it became more difficult to predict with certainty which actions of police, prosecutors, and judges were subject to constitutional limitations and which were not. The changing composition of the Court undoubtedly created some of the confusion. Thirty men occupied seats on the bench from 1930 to 1960; on occasion, it appeared there were at least as many opinions on questions of criminal process. During the period no majority of justices formed a stable block of votes on the relationship between state criminal procedures and the Fourteenth Amendment. Sometimes, the shift in opinion could be dramatic, as happened in 1949 when two liberal justices died within days of each other, both replaced by men of more conservative temperament.

This back and forth movement paralleled indecision elsewhere in the central government on issues touching the nationalization of rights. During World War II and the early Cold War, concern about internal security dominated the legislative and executive agendas. Both Congress and President hesitated to extend individual rights by statute or otherwise, especially when certain procedures—search and seizure, for example—seemed vital to the discovery of information, because to do so might restrain the campaign against subversion and disloyalty. The nascent civil rights movement also led to unresolved tensions among elected officials as southern whites once again raised the banner of state sovereignty in response to black demands for equal protection of their rights. Such spirited defense of local custom and a general reluctance to disturb the federal division of power undoubtedly influenced the Court's deferential attitude on matters of state criminal justice.

Whatever the reasons, continued adherence to the fair trial test exposed the Court to charges that defendant's rights depended on judicial caprice. Often the sharpest attacks came from dissenting justices who found the notion of fairness to be an inconsistent guide to the appeals before them. Decisions depended too much on judges' personal reactions to the facts presented by each case. Such an *ad hoc* approach, Chief Justice Warren cautioned in 1957, "is to build on shifting sands."[34] It was also at odds with the Court's decisions on First Amendment freedoms. These rights applied fully and identically to central and state governments alike under the due process clause of the Fourteenth Amendment. Why should not the same standard govern rights of the accused? *Palko* v. *Connecticut*, forebearer of the fair trial doctrine, contained no "license to the judiciary to administer a watered-down subjective version of the individual guarantees of the Bill of Rights."[35]

At times, advocates of the fair trial rule acknowledged these problems, although they argued that justice and federalism demanded it. The very nature of due process—the Constitution's "least specific and most comprehensive protection of liberties"—made it inevitable that judgement would "fall differently at different times and differently at the same time through different judges."[36] This result was natural. The whole development of due process rested on historical accidents of time and place, not on universal circumstances. Local values influenced, maybe determined, the meaning of justice. Federalism promoted such diversity; indeed, one of the strengths of the American constitutional order was the ability of states to try new ideas without risk to the nation-at-large. The fair trial interpretation of the due process clause best advanced this virtue, while ensuring that no state experimentation would deny citizens their fundamental liberty.

By the late 1950s four justices—Warren, Black, Douglas, and Brennan—were ready to abandon the fair trial approach to the Fourteenth Amendment. The 1960s witnessed their triumph. Too much had changed nationally to permit continuation of an interpretation that defined rights of the accused in terms of state boundaries. State prosecutors and local law enforcement alike had grown weary of a tribunal in distant Washington deciding long after trial that state practices used to convict were at odds with the U. S. Constitution. Law schools and bar associations too desired more uniform standards. Increasingly, commentators and legal scholars questioned why Amendments 4, 5, 6, and 8 were not equally as fundamental to national citizenship as economic liberties or the freedom to speech and press, rights long since subject to national jurisdiction.[37]

These concerns doubtless did not trouble most middle-class citizens. Prevention of crime—at least restricting it to less desirable areas—was always first on their minds. Few people violated the law, so the notion of rights remained an abstraction, at best a subject of civic pride. But in a nation where interstate highways collapsed distances and franchise restaurants erased a sense of place, it was only a matter of time before national standards replaced local practices.

For criminal law the shift came in a rush of Supreme Court cases during the 1960s and 1970s. In what was termed "the due process revolution," the Bill of Rights became a national code of criminal procedure. Suddenly, rights of criminal defendants became more real, more immediate, and for many people, more threatening. Once again, the Court was the storm center of American politics, but this time the promise of the past would be redeemed: the guarantees of the Bill of Rights would apply equally to all citizens everywhere.

6

JUDICIAL LIBERALISM AND THE DUE PROCESS REVOLUTION

Identifying the Supreme Court by the name of its chief justice is often misleading. By exaggerating the influence of one person, the label may obscure the importance of other justices in shaping constitutional interpretation. Or it may suggest a shift in judicial decisions that did not in fact occur. Yet at times the leadership of the chief justice so encourages new directions that his name becomes synonymous with the Court itself. Most chief justices do not earn the association, except as convenient shorthand. In the nineteenth century, scholars uniformly personify only the courts led by John Marshall and Roger B. Taney. For the twentieth century, there is a single example: Earl Warren.

Warren was a former California district prosecutor, attorney general, and governor whose appointment as Chief Justice in 1953 represented President Eisenhower's repayment of a political debt. Nothing marked Warren as a man of judicial temperament. He was instead an experienced politician. His philosophy and record classed him as a Progressive, intent on rooting out corruption and instilling order through vigorous law enforcement. He embraced the values of public morality, patriotism, and progress and championed active government administered by experts as the best means of securing a just society. Energy in government, he believed, came from the executive; the legislature he viewed as the venal handmaiden of special interests. The judiciary scarcely figured in his pre-Court calculus of proper government.[1] No wonder the conservative Eisenhower felt betrayed when Earl Warren led the Court through an extraordinarily controversial period, one that witnessed the triumph of judicial liberalism, the nationalization of the Bill of Rights, and an unprecedented expansion of the rights of criminal defendants.

Warren's tenure signaled a shift in judicial style from restraint to activism. Twentieth-century commentators long had rejected earlier notions of judges as mere oracles of the law, discovering principles unintelligible to laymen and applying them impartially to difficult cases. More recent theories recognized that judges made law, although this consequence proved troublesome to democratic government. Unrestrained judicial lawmaking threatened the idea of popular sovereignty. The problem was how to control an unelected bench; the solution lay in the judges' own good sense, manifested by respect for elected representatives and by rational and impartial decisions based on well-articulated reasons. Restraint was the watchword, and this principle guided several influential justices—Holmes, Brandeis, and Frankfurter, chief among them—as they sought an effective role for the Court. By mid-century, the expression of judicial restraint took more certain shape: deference to legislative actions, especially in matters of economic policy; respect for federalism and the diversity of state practice it implied; and reliance upon neutral decision-making based on narrow case facts rather than broad constitutional interpretation.[2]

As Chief Justice, Earl Warren rejected these canons of judging. His philosophy emerged from political experience, not academic study. Warren specifically dismissed as "fantasy" the notion that justices should be impartial. "As the defender of the Constitution," he wrote, "the Court cannot be neutral." He sought a broad role and active stance for the high bench: the "Court sits to decide cases, not to avoid decision, and while it must recognize the constitutional powers of the branches of Government involved, it must also decide every issue properly placed before it."[3]

More important, Court decisions must reach the right result, a condition defined by ethics, not legal procedures. Warren firmly believed the Constitution embodied moral truths that were essential to enlightened government. It was the Court's duty to apply these principles, even if doing so contravened the expressed wishes of the legislature. Warren was antagonistic to justices like Frankfurter who urged the Court to protect the integrity of democratic process and trust the people's representatives to promote liberty. Legislatures were too often the captives of special interests, he believed. The Court's role was to champion the individual, especially those citizens without a meaningful political voice.[4]

Nowhere was Warren's judicial philosophy more evident than in his attitude toward the Bill of Rights. In a 1955 essay, the Chief Justice outlined his understanding of American constitutional guarantees. The Bill of Rights, he argued, protected the natural rights of man against arbitrary actions of government. It codified the "sense of justice" inherent in human nature and provided the basis for bringing American law "more and more into harmony with moral principles." No legal doctrine curbed the protection of individual rights against the state, and no institutional limits encumbered judges in enforcing them.

These views required the "constant and creative application" of the Bill of Rights to new situations. "The pursuit of justice," Warren wrote, "is not the vain pursuit of remote abstraction." It was an active search for a fundamental morality to guide daily life, led by an independent judiciary. This process implied continual revision of the catalog of rights, leaving "a document that will not have exactly the same meaning it had when we received it from our fathers" but one that would be better because it was "burnished by growing use."[5]

By the 1960s the Court was ready to embrace Warren's activist stance. Three justices—Black, Douglas, and Brennan—joined with the Chief Justice to form a solid core of support for nationalizing the Bill of Rights. A changing fifth member, usually Clark, Goldberg, or Fortas, completed the majority. The leading advocate of federalism, Felix Frankfurter, dissented forcefully until his stroke and subsequent resignation in 1962. Then Justice John Marshall Harlan became the chief spokesman for the minority, a position that contrasted sharply with the unbending nationalism his grandfather, the earlier Justice Harlan, had voiced during a more conservative judicial era.

The cases differed from term to term, but the overarching goal of the Warren Court remained constant. At times with almost doctrinaire zeal, the justices sought to abolish distinctions of class and wealth in American society. Equality of condition joined equality of opportunity in the pantheon of modern liberal values the Court promoted. Liberty, long defined as the restraint of power, now required positive governmental action. Individual freedom no longer rested on the unbridled use of private property. The outstanding feature of post-New Deal constitutional law was the judicial abandonment of property rights to legislative and executive discretion and the subsequent defense of individual civil liberties. These rights, enumerated in the first eight amendments, became bedrock principles of modern judicial liberalism.[6]

The Court's new emphasis on equality and national standards was consistent with broader social and political developments. The United States had become an encompassing commercial society, with products pitched indiscriminately to all classes and regions. Network television and nationally circulated magazines spurred the growth of a homogeneous popular culture, which franchises, chain stores, and mass marketing exploited and reinforced. Customers at Sears or J. C. Penney, responding to the same advertisements, bought the same product at the same price, whether they shopped in Pittsburgh, Pennsylvania, or Phoenix, Arizona. McDonald's hamburgers tasted alike in Pratt, Kansas, and Phenix City, Alabama. Even the settings and decor varied little. Undoubtedly the democratization of the marketplace with its emphasis on uniformity prompted expectations of equal treatment, just as it dimmed belief in the values of diversity and difference.

Politically, the nation experienced a resurgence of liberalism in the 1960s under the presidencies of Kennedy and Johnson. This revival owed much to the Court's initiatives in civil rights. Beginning with *Brown* v. *Board of Education* (1954), decision after decision erased the legal distinctions that had buttressed a racially segregated society. Negroes became politically active and their demands for equality assumed high rank on the Democratic agenda. The Great Society failed to remedy discrimination or alleviate poverty, but its goals and programs lent credence nonetheless to the rhetoric of substantive equality, not merely the equal opportunity promised by earlier liberal reformers. Congressional action on behalf of a social and economic underclass both legitimated and sustained judicial activism directed toward common ends. For most of the decade, the justices who had sparked the movement for equality drew support from a liberal political coalition that preached a similar message.

Acting with unprecedented boldness during the 1960s, the majority justices of Warren Court promoted liberal policies they deemed essential to a just society. The reforms came so swiftly that many commentators proclaimed them revolutionary—and in some sense, they were. There was nothing new in the Court's method: conservative justices from 1890 to 1937 had often assumed power to make policy in defense of property rights. And the imposition of national standards on the states was a familiar constitutional refrain. What seemed fundamentally different was the vast range of issues addressed by the Court and the controversy its opinions stirred. There were sweeping decisions on the electoral process, political representation, school desegregation, public support of religion, obscenity, and free speech, among others—each one greeted by widespread public debate, often accompanied by angry threats to reverse the Court's action. But no judicial reforms were as bold or ignited more protest as the landmark cases involving criminal process. Nor in any other area were the results so revolutionary.

Between 1961 and 1969 the Warren Court accomplished what previous courts had stoutly resisted: it applied virtually all the procedural guarantees of the Bill of Rights to the states' administration of criminal justice. Adopting the strategy of selective incorporation, the justices explicitly defined the Fourteenth Amendment phrase, due process of law, to include most of the rights outlined in the Fourth, Fifth, and Sixth Amendments. The result was a nationalized Bill of Rights that dimmed the local character of justice by applying the same restraints to all criminal proceedings, both state and federal. The majority justices did not seek to diminish states' rights: they desired instead to elevate subminimal state practices to a higher national standard. But in the process, the Court reshaped the nature of federalism itself.

The first breakthrough occurred early in the decade as the Court extended the Fourth Amendment fully to the states. Previous to 1960 there were two limitations on constitutional protection against unreasonable searches. First, prosecutors could use illegally gained evidence to secure a conviction. *Wolf* v. *Colorado* (1949) had established the principle that the core of the Fourth Amendment, namely, its prohibition of unreasonable searches, applied equally to state and federal officials, but the justices refused to require state courts to adopt the federal exclusionary rule. Second, even federal courts, under the so-called silver platter doctrine, might permit the use of evidence obtained illegally by state officers in searches which involved neither federal participation nor federal direction. By 1961 the Court had removed both limitations, initially discarding the silver platter doctrine and then applying the exclusionary rule to state criminal trials.[7]

The *Wolf* decision cast doubt on the continuing viability of the silver platter doctrine, a result the Court seemed to recognize in several subsequent cases. In 1956, for example, the justices reversed a lower court decision that denied an injunction to prevent a federal agent from introducing tainted evidence in a state proceeding. Setting aside all constitutional questions, the Court ruled that federal policies forbade the agent's conduct. The rules were impotent "if the federal agent can flout them and use the fruits of his unlawful act either in federal or state proceedings."[8] But was the reverse true? Could federal courts continue to admit evidence obtained solely from illegal state searches, a practice permitted under the silver platter exception to the exclusionary rule?

Finally, in *Elkins* v. *United States* (1960), the justices abandoned the silver platter doctrine. Logic alone dictated the result. *Wolf* extended the constitutional prohibition against unreasonable searches to the states, yet federal courts accepted evidence gathered in violation of the Constitution. This practice threatened judicial integrity. Federal judges were "accomplices in the willful disobedience of the Constitution they are sworn to uphold." More important, the doctrine undermined federalism. Almost half the states had adopted the exclusionary rule, so "by admitting the unlawfully seized evidence the federal court serves to defeat the state's effort to assure obedience to the Federal Constitution."[9] It also frustrated state policy and promoted needless conflict between state and federal courts. The tables had turned on those justices who defended the silver platter doctrine out of respect for the federal principle.

The *Elkins* decision forecast a new relationship between the Fourth and Fourteenth Amendments—and between the state and federal governments. The Court required federal judges to use Fourth Amendment standards, including the exclusionary rule, to determine the admissibility of state evidence in federal trials. Why not go further and require state courts, like federal courts, to exclude unconstitutionally seized evidence? The next year the Court took this step.

In *Mapp* v. *Ohio* (1961) the Court applied the federal exclusionary rule to state criminal procedure. The case facts revealed a blatant disregard of search and seizure guarantees. Three Cleveland policemen, acting on an anonymous tip, went to the home of Dollree Mapp, seeking a fugitive wanted in a recent bombing incident. The suspect, they believed, also had gambling paraphernalia in his possession. Mapp refused entrance without a search warrant. For about three hours the policemen waited outside the apartment door, then upon the arrival of four other officers, they forced their way into the residence, waving a piece of paper they claimed was a search warrant. Mapp grabbed the paper and stuffed it into her dress; after a struggle, the officers retrieved it, handcuffed her, and locked her in a bedroom. The subsequent search left a ransacked apartment but produced neither the suspect nor the gambling equipment. It did turn up pornographic material, however. Although she claimed that it had been left by a previous tenant, Mapp was convicted on an obscenity charge and sentenced to prison. The Ohio Supreme Court affirmed the conviction because state law permitted the use of illegally seized evidence.[10]

By a narrow 5–4 vote, the U. S. Supreme Court disagreed. The full Fourth Amendment applied to the states, Justice Clark wrote in the prevailing opinion. And with the amendment's protection went the means to enforce it, the federal exclusionary rule. "To hold otherwise," he reasoned, "is to grant the right but in reality to withhold its privilege and enjoyment." Any other decision was also harmful to healthy federal-state relations. The lack of an exclusionary policy in many states only "encourage[d] disobedience" to constitutional standards as federal officers "step across the street" to deliver illegally seized evidence to local police and prosecutors. A common exclusionary rule would promote federal-state cooperation "if only by recognition of their now mutual obligation to respect the same fundamental criteria in their approach." The decision would not impede effective law enforcement, but if it did, the Constitution was more important. "Nothing can destroy a government more quickly," Clark concluded, "than its failure to observe its own laws, or worse, its disregard of the charter of its own existence."[11]

Suddenly the barrier against selective incorporation of the criminal safeguards of the Bill of Rights had fallen. The margin was slim, but the abandonment of the fair trial interpretation of constitutional guarantees was unmistakable. Dissenting justices recognized the shift and in defeat raised an objection that accompanied subsequent advances in the due process revolution. The Court, they charged, had exceeded its authority. Justice Harlan, rapidly becoming spokesman for his more conservative colleagues, bluntly stated his concern: "[T]his Court can increase respect for the Constitution only if it rigidly respects the limitations which the Constitution places upon it, and respects as well the principles inherent in its own processes. In the present case I think we exceed both, and that our voice becomes only a voice of power, not reason."[12]

The Court had acted uncharacteristically, although in a manner symbolic of future cases. Not only did the majority justices abruptly jettison an interpretive posture that had guided decisions since 1937—and discard an even earlier doctrinal separation of state and federal criminal power—they went beyond the positions taken by opposing counsel in oral arguments before the bench. With both actions, the Court openly fashioned its decision on the majority's sense of a right result. The process exposed the justices to public criticism that they had usurped legislative and executive authority.

The issue was not merely the abandonment of established doctrine. Overturning a precedent was uncommon but not unknown. Few jurists or commentators believed in absolute *stare decisis,* that is, in following slavishly the principles established in earlier decisions. Much more troublesome was the justices' willingness to reverse a precedent when it was not even in dispute before them. The counsel for Mapp did not ask the Court to overrule *Wolf* v. *Colorado,* although the justices squarely asked him about it during oral arguments. Nor did he cite the *Wolf* precedent in his brief; astonishingly, he was not even aware of it. Other briefs ignored the case. Every party argued the appeal on First, not Fourth, Amendment grounds; the American Civil Liberties Union alone, in one paragraph, urged the Court to overturn *Wolf.* Yet the Court's opinion ignored freedom of speech, a right already applied to the states, and focused instead on the reach of the Fourth Amendment. No matter how explained, the decision buttressed Justice Harlan's claim that the majority "simply 'reached out' to overrule" *Wolf.* Liberal judicial activists, despite their trenchant criticism of earlier attempts to legislate social and economic policy from the bench, were in turn vulnerable to the same charge.[13]

The next year, 1962, the Court employed the same tactic in extending the Eighth Amendment to the states. Under challenge was a section of the California health and safety code that made narcotics addiction a misdemeanor punishable by fine and imprisonment. By a vote of 6 to 2, the justices declared the law unconstitutional. Crimes involve illegal acts, they reasoned; drug addiction, while it may result from prohibited conduct, is a condition or status, not an act. A statute making a disease a criminal offense, such as imprisoning someone because he was an addict, was "an infliction of cruel and unusual punishment in violation of the Eighth and Fourteenth Amendments."[14]

Once again the Court had determined that the Fourteenth Amendment's due process clause incorporated a protection found in the Bill of Rights. The states too were bound by the prohibition of cruel and unusual punishments. Equally significant was the justices' willingness to go beyond the issues framed by the pleadings before them: in briefs and oral argument the application of the Eighth Amendment to the states received only passing notice. It was becoming apparent that an activist majority controlled the Court, one intent on expanding the catalog of defendants' rights and applying it uniformly across the nation.

This new direction became certain one year later when the Court unanimously declared that the Sixth Amendment right to counsel in criminal cases applied to the states under the due process clause of the Fourteenth Amendment. Reflecting upon *Gideon* v. *Wainwright* (1963) after his retirement, former Chief Justice Warren viewed it as one of the most important decisions made during his tenure.[15] Few scholars would disagree. Its significance was two-fold: it extended an important federal guarantee to state criminal defendants; and it marked the triumph of the incorporationists over fair trial advocates in determining the meaning of the Bill of Rights.

Clarence Earl Gideon was a fifty-year-old drifter and former convict when he was arrested in 1961 for breaking and entering a Panama City, Florida, poolroom with intent to commit petty larceny. Upon trial the judge refused his request for counsel, ruling that Florida law made court-appointed attorneys available only to defendants charged with capital crimes. The state supreme court in turn, following the U.S. Supreme Court's decision in *Betts* v. *Brady* (1942), rejected his handwritten appeal because he did not fit the special circumstances that required appointment of counsel in noncapital cases: he was literate, mature, knowledgeable about court procedure, and the judge and prosecutor had not taken advantage of him. Still, Gideon insisted that he had a constitutional right to an attorney.[16] In 1963 the nation's highest court agreed.

The justices were unanimous: *Betts* v. *Brady* was an error. Instead of following the lead of *Powell* v. *Alabama,* the famous Scottsboro case that required counsel for indigent capital defendants, the Court in 1942 had made "an abrupt break with its own well-considered precedents." The due process clause of the Fourteenth Amendment required states to adopt provisions of the Bill of Rights that were fundamental and essential to a fair trial, Justice Black wrote in the Court's opinion. And a defendant "who is too poor to hire a lawyer, cannot be assured a fair trial unless counsel is provided for him. This seems to us to be an obvious truth."[17]

Black's opinion employed fair trial rhetoric but the Court's preeminent advocate of total incorporation had not abandoned his long-held position that the complete Bill of Rights applied to the states by means of the Fourteenth Amendment. Incorporationist language was not necessary. The result was the same regardless of the interpretive guide—fair trial or incorporation—chosen by individual justices. Black simply took an approach that accommodated both positions, thus ensuring unanimity.

Still, the opinion clearly represented a major victory for incorporationists. What made this conclusion inescapable were twenty-three *amicus curiae,* or friend-of-the-court, briefs from state attorneys general asking the justices to impose a uniform rule on state and federal courts alike. For over two decades the prevailing fair trial view had justified the case-by-case determination of due process and the resulting diversity of state practice as a necessary requirement of federalism. Now the states' chief lawyers wanted the Court to mandate the assistance of counsel in all serious criminal cases. Their assessment of the fair trial approach to defendants' rights was damning. It had resulted only in "twenty years' accumulation of confusion and contradictions" that failed totally "as a beacon to guide trial judges."[18] The states themselves, it appeared, were ready for the nationalization of this important right.

The next year, 1964, the incorporationist majority added yet another element to the growing list of federal criminal procedures applied to the states. The Fifth Amendment protection against self-incrimination, the Court concluded, 5–4, in *Malloy* v. *Hogan,* was part of the due process clause of the Fourteenth Amendment.[19] The decision reversed another long-standing precedent: *Twining* v. *New Jersey* (1908) had determined the right against self-incrimination to be only a valued rule of evidence, not an essential part of due process.

More important was the Court's explicit recognition of the theory of selective incorporation in justification of its decision. *Twining* had established the rule that rights embodied in the due process clause were similar to, not the same as, the guarantees of the first eight amendments, a principle embraced by later justices who favored the fair trial interpretation of the Fourteenth Amendment. Now the Court announced a new doctrine: rights found to be incorporated in the due process clause of the Fourteenth Amendment were identical to corresponding guarantees of the Bill of Rights. "[I]t would be incongruous," Justice Brennan wrote for the majority, "to have different standards" for state and federal courts when judging claims of protection under the self-incrimination clause. The Fourteenth Amendment did not extend a "watered down, subjective version of the Bill of Rights" to the states.[20] Henceforth states must apply federal self-incrimination standards. The privilege carried the same meaning in all jurisdictions; the right was national in scope.

The Court's rejection of *Twining* and its more general interpretation of due process was not unexpected. In First Amendment cases since 1947 the Court had applied the same standards to states and federal government alike. Nonetheless, the concept of identical meaning in criminal procedure marked a significant advance for advocates of selective incorporation. Justice Harlan recognized this shift and registered his disapproval in a biting dissent. Brennan's opinion, he charged, had distorted the historical development of due process by pretending its guarantees were the same as the rights listed in the first eight amendments. Even worse, the majority incorporationists had broken well-established bounds of judicial restraint. They had taken the Fourteenth Amendment's due process clause as "short-hand directive . . . to pick and choose among the [Bill of Rights] . . . and apply those chosen, freighted with their entire accompanying body of federal doctrine, to law enforcement in the States." The result damaged the federal system by establishing a national guide for problems best left to state discretion. "The Court's reference to a federal standard is, to put it bluntly, simply an excuse to substitute its own superficial assessment of the facts and state law for the careful and better informed conclusions of the state court."[21]

Harlan's remarks went unheeded. The incorporationists now commanded a majority on the Court, thanks to new appointments to the bench. Eventual nationalization of defendants' rights seemed inevitable. In a decision in 1963, the year previous to the *Malloy* decision, the Court had extended all federal standards on search and seizure to the actions of state law enforcement. Now, federal rules governed trial court decisions on issues regarding self-incrimination. The next year, 1965, in *Pointer* v. *Texas,* the Court ruled that "the Sixth Amendment right of an accused to confront the witnesses against him is a fundamental right and is made obligatory on the States by the Fourteenth Amendment."[22]

The case involved the testimony of a witness who had since moved out of state. Could the trial court accept evidence from his preliminary examination, an occasion when the accused was without counsel, in lieu of attendance at the trial itself? Texas law permitted it; the U. S. Supreme Court decided otherwise. Although the defendant's attorney was present at trial, the opportunity had passed for cross-examination of the absent witness; as Chief Justice Warren commented in oral arguments, "you can't unring a bell."[23] Texas procedure violated the Sixth and Fourteenth Amendments. The defendant's ability to confront witnesses against him, like the protection against self-incrimination, was a national right, and federal rules governed its practice in all state courts.

The liberal majority had chosen a course of selectively incorporating the procedural guarantees of the Bill of Rights, but by what rationale? Although the incorporationist justices never advanced a systematic theory, Justice Goldberg's concurring opinion in *Pointer* offered an explanation of their logic. The fair trial approach, rather than preserving federalism as its defenders maintained, had actually subverted healthy relations between the states and central government because its case-by-case decisions invited "haphazard and unpredictable intrusions by the federal judiciary in state proceedings." Yet much more was at stake than the federal principle, even though it too, as Justice Harlan reminded his colleagues, was "constitutionally ordained." States might properly experiment in social or economic policy without harm to the nation, Goldberg asserted. This characteristic was a virtue of the federal system. But there could be no "power to experiment with the fundamental liberties of citizens." Diversity here threatened liberty by requiring the Court "to make the extremely subjective and excessively discretionary determination as to whether a practice . . . is . . . sufficiently repugnant to the notion of due process as to be forbidden the States."[24] Selective incorporation, in sum, promoted federalism, restrained unwarranted judicial discretion, and ensured equal justice.

A surprisingly muted public response greeted the Court's early decisions on criminal procedure. News coverage of the landmark cases was limited, and, except for the exclusionary rule, few commentators made the changes an issue for extended discussion. The civil rights movement, and the cases resulting from it, made far more dramatic and compelling claims on public attention. Especially telling was the lack of response by the states or their representatives. By the 1960s there existed several national organizations, notably the National Association of State Attorneys General and the National District Attorneys Association, which expressed and defended state interests before the federal courts. Yet the most significant intervention by these groups occurred in *Gideon* v. *Wainwright* when the attorneys general of twenty-three states supported the imposition of a national standard. The Court's decisions may have caught states by surprise; several important opinions—*Mapp* v. *Ohio* and *Pointer* v. *Texas,* for example—rested on lines of reasoning not mooted in briefs or oral arguments before the justices. More likely was the states' general agreement with the Court's direction. Uniform rules, at least the ones announced by 1965, did not threaten the core of state power, and they removed much of the uncertainty that accompanied numerous appeals.[25]

Only state judges made any sustained criticism of the Court's dramatic intrusion into the area of criminal justice. State supreme court justices in particular expressed strong disapproval. Thirty-two of the fifty highest state tribunals voiced disagreement with one or more of the nationalizing cases, usually *Mapp.* Even so, the protests remained few in number. State courts implemented the new policies without comment in 95 percent of the applicable cases. Ironically, the sharpest dissent from state judges came in the 1950s, under the fair trial regime, when the Conference of State Chief Justices endorsed a resolution criticizing ''the extent of the control over the actions of the states which the Supreme Court exercises under its views of the Fourteenth Amendment.''[26]

The scant public attention given to the nationalization of defendant's rights disappeared abruptly in 1966 when the Court tackled the politically controversial task of reforming the states' pre-trial procedures. *Miranda* v. *Arizona* ignited a firestorm of criticism. At issue was the admissibility of confessions obtained during police interrogations in which the suspect had not been told of his right to consult an attorney or to remain silent. There were several relevant precedents. The Court in 1936, in *Brown* v. *Mississippi,* held that a coerced confession brought about by police torture was a violation of the due process clause of the Fourteenth Amendment. More recently, two cases decided by the Warren Court— *Spano* v. *New York* (1959) and *Escobedo* v. *Illinois* (1964)—had invalidated confessions gained as a result of extended police questioning without the suspect's attorney being present. The ruling in *Escobedo* especially—that police could not deny access to an attorney—pointed directly to the result announced in *Miranda:* the Fifth Amendment protection against self-incrimination extended to suspects under interrogation by the police.[27]

Chief Justice Warren's opinion for the Court was a classic expression of his ethically based, result-oriented jurisprudence. The opinion first detailed the unfair and forbidding nature of police interrogations. Police manuals and comments by law enforcement officials revealed that beatings, intimidation, psychological pressure, false statements, and denial of food and sleep were standard techniques used to secure the suspect's confession. For Warren these tactics suggested that "the interrogation environment [existed] . . . for no purpose other than to subjugate the individual to the will of his examiner."[28] Ethics alone made reprehensible any practice that tricked or cajoled suspects from exercising their constitutional rights, leaving them dependent, isolated, abandoned, and vulnerable. But such police tactics also violated the Fifth Amendment protection against self-incrimination, although the precedents cited in support of this position did not involve custodial interrogation. In fact, one case offered in justification, *Escobedo* v. *Illinois,* addressed the Sixth, not the Fifth, Amendment.

By far the longest part of the opinion was a detailed code of police conduct. The new rules quickly became familiar to anyone who watched crime dramas on television: the suspect must be informed that he has the right to remain silent; that anything he says can and will be used against him in court; that he has the right to have counsel present during questioning; and that if he cannot afford an attorney, the court will appoint a lawyer to represent him. These privileges took effect from the first instance of police interrogation while the suspect was "in custody at the station or otherwise deprived of his freedom in any significant way." And the rights could be waived only "knowingly and intelligently," a condition presumed not to exist if lengthy questioning preceded the required warnings.[29]

Warren's language vividly portrayed the unequal relationship between interrogator and suspect, an imbalance that the Chief Justice believed did not belong in a democratic society. "The prosecutor under our system," he commented later, "is not paid to convict people [but to] protect the rights of people . . . and to see that when there is a violation of the law, it is vindicated by trial and prosecution under fair judicial standards."[30] The presence of a lawyer and a protected right of silence created a more equal situation for the accused; thus, these conditions were essential to the constitutional conception of fairness.

Police officers, prosecutors, commentators, and politicians were quick to denounce the *Miranda* warnings. Critics charged that recent Court decisions, culminating with *Escobedo* and *Miranda,* had "handcuffed" police efforts to fight crime. This claim found a receptive audience among a majority of the general public worried about rising crime rates, urban riots, racial conflict, and the counterculture's challenge to middle-class values. Politicians eager to curry votes joined the chorus of protest. "Support your local police" became a familiar campaign slogan for candidates who sought electoral advantage in opposing the Court's reforms of pre-trial procedure. The belief that the *Miranda* decision threatened public safety even acquired a certain legitimacy from members of the Supreme Court itself. "[I]n some unknown number of cases," Justice White warned in dissent to Warren's majority opinion, "the Court's rule will return a killer, a rapist or other criminal to the streets . . . to repeat his crime whenever it pleases him."[31]

The police response to *Miranda* was predictable but exaggerated. Numerous studies have since demonstrated that the decision, like the ones in *Mapp* and *Escobedo,* did not restrain the police unduly and, in fact, had little effect on the disposition of most cases. The reason lay in the nature of police work. Much law enforcement necessarily occurs without supervision. Who was to determine whether policemen followed court-mandated procedures in conducting investigations? Trial judges and prosecutors, the logical supervisors, often were elected officials sensitive to public demands to punish criminals. Suspects also were inadequate monitors because they commonly waived their rights, especially the right to remain silent (silence evidently is an unnatural posture for one accused of crime), and willingly cooperated with the police, hoping in turn to secure more lenient treatment. Neither did the presence of attorneys ensure compliance with the new rules. Access to an attorney, usually an overworked and underpaid public defender, may have smoothed negotiations between suspect and prosecutor, but it did not lessen the percentage of cases resolved by plea bargains nor did it result in more dismissals or cases going to trial.[32]

At the time these things went unnoticed. What everyone recognized instead was the dramatic rise in crime and disorder. There was indeed a rapid growth in the incidence of reported crime, but the Supreme Court did not cause it. Rather, the baby boom generation had come of age. Young males, ages 15 to 24, traditionally account for most violations of law, and it was this group that now composed a larger-than-usual percentage of the nation's population. *Miranda* rules or not, there would be more crime. Police critics of the Court, frustrated by public demands to do something, simply found the Supreme Court a convenient scapegoat for their own inability to contain the explosive increase in criminal behavior.

Although controversial, the *Miranda* decision—and to some extent the *Mapp* and *Escobedo* cases that preceded it—gradually brought needed improvements in police practices. Police procedures came more fully into public view, resulting in heightened awareness of official misconduct and greater expectations of professionalism. In response, many police departments raised standards for employment, adopted performance guidelines, and improved training and supervision.[33] The Court's actions had begun to bear fruit, much in the manner desired by the majority who believed that hard work and respect for the law, not deception or law-breaking, were the requirements of effective law enforcement.

Significantly, the Court did not stand alone in its effort to reform pretrial criminal process. At the time of the *Miranda* decision, some state legislatures had already mandated stricter rules for custodial interrogation, and the subject was under study by several professional and governmental commissions. The American Law Institute had completed a draft of a Model Code of Pre-Arraignment Procedure, and the newly created President's Commission on Law Enforcement and the Administration of Justice had as one of its goals the reform of criminal procedures.[34] Paradoxically, the Court's *Miranda* decision slowed attempts to strengthen defendants' rights by revising criminal codes, at least to the degree that people associated judicially mandated procedures with increased crime. Imposition of sweeping guidelines by the nation's highest bench had the obvious advantage of immediate and uniform application, but it also short-circuited the legislative process, a step that, if followed, might have defused some of the issue's political volatility.

The Court, ever aware of public criticism, did make concessions to ensure more widespread acceptance of its actions. Most important was its decision not to apply new rulings retroactively. Prisoners convicted under older, discredited procedures would not be granted new trials simply because the Court now found those policies unconstitutional. The justices acknowledged that applying rules to future cases alone might benefit some defendants, while denying equal treatment to prisoners convicted under abandoned procedures. But they admitted candidly that wholesale release of prisoners in pursuit of equal justice was politically unacceptable. Public acceptance of controversial decisions, the majority justices evidently concluded, was made easier by limiting their application.[35]

The Court also hesitated to restrict the police unduly. In 1966, the same year as the *Miranda* decision, it held that the government's use of decoys, undercover agents, and hired informers to gain evidence of crime was not necessarily unconstitutional. The justices further approved the admissibility of information secured by wiretaps. The next year the Court accepted as constitutional a warrantless arrest in a narcotics case based upon the word of an informer who the prosecution refused to identify in a pre-trial hearing. And in a Fourth Amendment case the justices sustained the right of police "in hot pursuit" of a suspect to search a house and seize incriminating evidence without a warrant.[36]

These moderating decisions failed to quiet the Court's critics, but mounting pressure did not deter the justices from making further reforms in state criminal procedures. *In re Gault* extended certain due process requirements of the Bill of Rights to juvenile courts.[37] Several important decisions incorporated the remaining Sixth Amendment guarantees—specifically, the rights to compulsory process, speedy trial, and trial by jury—into the due process clause of the Fourteenth Amendment, thus creating new restraints on state criminal process. The Court continued to insist that poverty should be no impediment to justice by requiring the state to furnish transcripts to indigent defendants. And it maintained its long-established position that confessions be truly voluntary.[38]

The cases, in hindsight, hardly appear controversial, but at the time they departed significantly from the decades-old tradition that defined criminal justice as a local responsibility. The Court, for example, unanimously struck down a part of the Texas Code of Criminal Procedure that prohibited codefendants from testifying on behalf of one another but allowed the state to call a codefendant as a prosecution witness.[39] In another case the unanimous justices determined that North Carolina's refusal to prosecute a criminal indictment against a civil rights' advocate kept the defendant in legal limbo and violated the Sixth Amendment's guarantee of speedy trial.[40] And in an appeal from Louisiana, the justices rejected the right of a state to withhold jury trial for defendants charged with serious offenses.[41]

The jury trial case, *Duncan* v. *Louisiana* (1968), in particular underscored the dramatically changed relationship between the federal Bill of Rights and the states' authority to establish criminal procedures. Earlier Courts had accepted state experimentation with any element of due process unless the justices considered it essential to a scheme of ordered liberty. This standard permitted the states to define fairness in a variety of ways, and these definitions, the Court concluded, may or may not include such traditional guarantees as jury trial for all serious offenses. But Justice White's opinion for the majority in *Duncan* rejected theory and diversity in favor of history and uniformity: "state criminal processes are not imaginary and theoretical schemes but actual systems bearing virtually every characteristic of the common-law system that has been developed in England and this country." The issue, White continued, was not whether a procedure is "fundamental to fairness in every criminal system that might be imagined but is fundamental in the context of the criminal processes maintained by the American states."[42] Jury trials were essential to Anglo-American justice, and therefore the Sixth Amendment guarantee applied to the states under the due process clause of the Fourteenth Amendment.

Outside of law journals, these later cases brought only scattered protest. Evidently most people accepted the Court's premise that rights of the accused were national in scope. Far more controversial were decisions like *Miranda* which defined these rights by proscribing certain police practices. Several cases in 1967 brought especially bitter criticism from "law and order" advocates and propelled the Court once again to the fore of American politics. The justices struck down a New York eavesdropping law under which police could obtain permission to tap or bug conversations without identifying the crime suspected or the evidence sought. The decision, based on the Fourth Amendment's prohibition of unreasonable searches, undermined similar laws in other states and, according to law enforcement officials, deprived them of yet another valuable crimefighting tool.[43]

The charge that the Court was coddling criminals gained momentum when, on the same day, the Court extended the right to counsel to suspects in a police lineup. In another case, *Katz* v. *United States*, the justices reversed the conviction of a gambler based on evidence gained by the warrantless bugging of a public telephone booth. The Fourth Amendment, Justice Marshall wrote, extended to persons, not places, thus abandoning the precedent that limited its protection only to physical spaces.[44] Forgotten in the rush to criticize the Court were other decisions that endorsed law enforcement values, such as several 1968 cases upholding a police officer's right to stop and frisk a suspect, admittedly a personal search within the Fourth Amendment meaning, and even to seize evidence without a warrant, so long as the officer's actions were reasonable under the circumstances.[45]

By 1968 the Court's due process revolution was nearing its end. Republican Presidential nominee Richard Nixon and third-party candidate George Wallace campaigned on strong "law and order" themes, pledging to restore a conservative cast to the Supreme Court if elected. Nixon, in particular, emphasized judicial permissiveness as a cause of crime: "All across the land," he claimed, "guilty men walk free from hundreds of courtrooms. Something has gone terribly wrong in America." Other politicians agreed. Stung by rioting in the streets of Detroit and Newark in 1967 and pressured by middle-class voters to curb the violence associated with racial tensions and anti-war protests, Congress responded by enacting the most extensive anticrime legislation in American history.

The Omnibus Crime Control and Safe Streets Act of 1968 contained a number of provisions designed to reverse recent Court decisions, especially the *Miranda* rule. Voluntary confessions were made admissible as evidence even if suspects had not been informed of their constitutional rights, with the trial judge to determine the issue of voluntariness out of the jury's hearing. Police could detain suspects for up to six hours or longer without arraignment if circumstances warranted it and still acquire an admissible confession. The act also made the use of wiretaps much easier in federal investigations.[46] Despite protests that these measures were unconstitutional, popular opinion clearly supported the Congressional action, even though the act did not apply to the states and thus had a limited impact. There had been too much disorder, too many killings and assassinations, too much property destroyed. Order, not rights, was the new public watchword.

The Supreme Court could not long ignore this shift in support for its reform of criminal justice, but first the Warren Court, in 1969, completed its due process revolution by reversing, fittingly, the landmark case that had justified state experimentation with criminal procedures, *Palko* v. *Connecticut*. The issue, as it had been in 1937, was double jeopardy. The question: did the Fifth Amendment prohibition restrain the states? Again, the answer was yes. Writing for the majority in *Benton* v. *Maryland*, Justice Marshall noted that the Court's recent cases had thoroughly rejected Justice Cardozo's premise in *Palko* that a denial of fundamental fairness rested on the total circumstances of a criminal proceeding, not simply one element of it. Once the Court decides a particular guarantee is fundamental to American justice, he continued, then failure to honor that safeguard is a denial of due process. Equally important, these essential protections applied uniformly to all jurisdictions. Rights of the accused did not vary from state to state; they were truly national rights.[47]

In a dual sense, the *Benton* case signaled the end of an era: it concluded the Warren Court's nationalization of the Bill of Rights, and it marked Earl Warren's retirement from the nation's highest bench. The Chief Justice and his liberal associates on the bench left an undeniable legacy. Never before had a group of judges championed so vigorously the rights of social outcasts—racial minorities, dissidents, the poor, and criminal defendants. Never before had the Court given such substantive meaning to the time-honored ethic of equal justice under law. No longer did the expression and application of rights depend so much on accidents of geography. In 1961 only eight of twenty-six provisions of the Bill of Rights restrained both federal and state governments; by 1969 only seven guarantees remained unincorporated in the Fourteenth Amendment, thus restricting the central government alone.

Most of the safeguards nationalized under decisions of the Warren Court were rights of the accused. In a brief eight years, the liberal majority had revolutionized the concept of criminal due process. But the expansion of rights was highly controversial, especially among state and local officials charged with law enforcement. Once more the Court occupied the center stage of American politics. The 1968 election of a conservative law-and-order candidate, Richard Nixon, as president foreshadowed an attempt to undo much of what the liberal justices had accomplished. Now the question was, would the revolution hold?

7

RIGHTS OF THE ACCUSED
IN A CONSERVATIVE AGE

On Earl Warren's last day as chief justice in June 1969, Richard Nixon made a rare presidential visit to the Supreme Court. He offered tribute to the retiring jurist, but his primary purpose was to introduce Warren's successor. Warren Earl Burger, previously on the Court of Appeals for the District of Columbia, had a reputation as a "law and order" judge with little sympathy for the Court's due process revolution. His appointment redeemed candidate Nixon's pledge to restore a conservative cast to the nation's highest bench, especially when a few years later three other appointees replaced Warren Court justices. But contrary to expectations, there was no counter-revolution in the law governing defendants' rights. Upon Burger's retirement in 1986, the major criminal procedure decisions of the Warren Court remained essentially intact.

The lasting influence of the due process revolution owed little to the new Chief Justice. Burger did not share his predecessor's concern for rights of the accused. He had often attacked the Court's procedural reforms while on the appellate bench, at one point claiming that recent decisions made guilt or innocence "irrelevant in the criminal trial as we flounder in a morass of artificial rules poorly conceived and often impossible of application." His announced goal was to limit the Court's rule-making intrusions into areas more properly reserved for the federal and state legislatures and to manage more efficiently the Court's large caseload.[1]

Revealing differences between Warren and Burger emerged in separate public interviews each man gave, coincidentally, two years after assuming the chief justiceship. In 1955 Warren maintained that the Court had a crucial responsibility to renew and fulfill the highest ideals of the Constitution, most notably the expressions of justice found in the Bill of Rights. The problem always was "how to apply to ever changing conditions the never changing principles of freedom." A more specific concern was reforming criminal process, a system riddled with "procedural flaws and anachronisms," to achieve truly equal justice under law.[2]

Burger in 1971 saw a more limited role for the Court. The justices sat simply to decide cases, not to make rules or create new law. Reform was properly the responsibility of the legislature. Some changes inevitably followed from court decisions, Burger admitted, but "to try to create or substantially change civil or criminal procedure, for example, by judicial decision is the worse possible way to do it." Above all the Court should approach matters cautiously: "legal principle can't be sound if its growth is too fast." What was the greatest challenge before the Court? "[T]o try to keep up with the volume of work and maintain the kind of quality" expected of the justices, Burger answered.[3] Significantly, the Bill of Rights merited not a word in the interview.

Even with the dissimilarity in judicial philosophy and temperament—a difference heightened by the appointment of more conservative justices during the 1970s and 1980s—the Court under new leadership did not renounce the due process revolution. But the justices were more tolerant of police behavior and less receptive to further expansion of rights for criminal defendants. Symbolic of the change was the Court's treatment of the Fourth Amendment's requirement for a search warrant. Previous decisions had challenged the validity of a warrant issued on the basis of rumors or even an anonymous informer's tip, yet in *United States* v. *Harris* (1971) a divided Court held that a suspect's reputation alone was sufficient to support a warrant application. Writing for the majority, Chief Justice Burger denounced "mere hypertechnicality" in warrant affidavits and urged a return to more practical considerations in actions against criminals.[4]

Subsequent cases confirmed the Court's new direction. The justices applied a much less restrictive interpretation to the probable cause requirement for granting a search warrant; they accepted a warrantless search as voluntary based on all the circumstances of the case rather than on an individual's knowledgeable consent; and they permitted illegally seized evidence to be presented to a grand jury even though it was inadmissible at trial. The Court also approved the "stop and frisk" practices of state and local police and allowed law officers broad latitude to search automobiles, even accepting in a narcotics case evidence seized from the car's passenger compartment without a warrant.[5]

Not only did the Court lower the threshold requirements for a valid search, it redefined the exclusionary rule. First applied to federal trials in *Weeks* v. *United States* (1914) and extended to the states in *Mapp* v. *Ohio* (1961), this doctrine prevented the use in court of evidence seized in an unconstitutional search. Framers of the exclusionary rule may have expected it to influence police behavior, but the principle itself, they believed, was part of the Fourth Amendment. Not so, concluded the Court in 1974. In ruling that grand jury witnesses may not use unlawful searches to excuse them from testifying, the Court characterized the exclusionary rule as a "judicially created remedy designed to safeguard Fourth Amendment rights generally through its deterrent effect." It was not a "personal constitutional right," and its use presented "a question, not of rights but of remedies"—one that should be answered by weighing the costs of the rule against its benefits.[6]

For a decade the Court invoked its new cost-benefit analysis cautiously, declining to apply it fully and directly to criminal prosecutions. But in 1984 the justices decided in *United States* v. *Leon* that evidence produced by an officer's reasonable or good faith reliance on the validity of a search warrant was admissible in court, even if the warrant later proved defective. The "good faith" exception to the exclusionary rule rested explicitly on a balancing of the costs and benefits involved: using evidence captured innocently under a defective warrant exacted a small price from Fourth Amendment protection when compared to the substantial cost society would bear if an otherwise guilty defendant went free. Although the exception applied only to the small percentage of police searches conducted under a warrant, opponents of the decision worried that, over time, the Court would render the exclusionary rule impotent if it invited a more casual approach to law enforcement.[7] The concern was not misplaced. Since the 1960s, strict adherence to the rule has resulted in improved police work, with evidence excluded or prosecutions dropped in less than 2 percent of all cases because of Fourth Amendment violations.[8]

If the justices in the 1970s and 1980s shifted the direction of Fourth Amendment decisions, they did not abandon entirely an earlier concern for rights of the accused. The Court declared unconstitutional a New

York law permitting police to conduct a warrantless search of a private home in order to make a felony arrest. It also prohibited a warrantless search of an automobile luggage compartment and required law officers to show probable cause of crime to check driver's licenses and auto registrations, although a later case lowered this threshold to "only a probability or substantial chance of criminal activity."[9] More important, the new conservative majority left undisturbed the Warren Court's signal contribution on search and seizure issues, namely, that Fourth Amendment standards applied equally to state and federal jurisdictions.

In most other areas of criminal procedure, the Court maintained but did little to advance the rights of the accused extended during the Warren era. Arguing that the law requires only a fair trial, not a perfect one, the Court upheld a conviction even though the police, when giving the required *Miranda* warnings, neglected to tell the defendant of his right to appointed counsel if he could not afford one. It also allowed admissions secured without the required warnings to be used to impeach the defendant's credibility, though not to obtain his conviction, if he took the stand on his own behalf. In Sixth Amendment cases the Court guaranteed the right to counsel to all trials that could lead to imprisonment; but following the lead of Congress in the Crime Control Act of 1968, it refused to grant the protection to unindicted suspects in a police lineup. Similarly, the justices extended the guarantee of a jury trial to include all petty misdemeanors punishable by six months or longer imprisonment, yet they allowed states to experiment with the size of juries and to allow 10–2 and 9–3 verdicts in non-capital cases.[10]

Only in cases involving the death penalty did the Court in the 1970s move beyond the Warren Court's conception of defendants' rights. Few constitutional phrases have fostered as much controversy as the Eighth Amendment's prohibition of "cruel and unusual punishment." Adopted when executions were common, the amendment's language—and comparable wording in all state constitutions—suggested reform, or so claimed the opponents of capital punishment in several nineteenth-century campaigns to remove the penalty from criminal law. Although a few states banned the punishment in the 1850s and 1860s, most legislatures only moved the gallows indoors, making executions private affairs rather than public spectacles.

The twentieth century witnessed a revival of the crusade against the death penalty, prompted by the widely publicized execution of defendants following highly controversial trials. But the focus shifted to the courts, not the legislature. Advocates of abolition, led by the ACLU and the NAACP, sought to persuade judges that capital punishment was cruel and unusual because it applied disproportionately to the poor, blacks, and members of unpopular groups and because it did not accomplish the two main ends of punishment, deterrence and rehabilitation. The evidence was unmistakable: countless studies documented the discriminatory impact of the death penalty; none found a strong statistical relationship between executions and the homicide rate.[11] The death penalty, opponents argued, was by definition cruel and unusual punishment; in practice, it was a denial of equal justice.

All federal and state courts in the 1960s accepted the constitutionality of capital punishment, but late in the decade a new focus for the debate began to emerge in the nation's courts. In 1968 the Supreme Court prohibited states from excluding opponents of executions from service as jurors in capital cases, although the justices otherwise refused to label the death penalty as cruel and unusual punishment. The Court of Appeals for the Fourth Circuit ruled in 1970 that the death penalty for rape was excessive, a position supported by recommendations from the National Commission on Reform of Federal Criminal Laws and the Model Penal Code. That same year the United States Congress abolished capital punishment for rape in the District of Columbia.[12]

Then in 1972 the Supreme Court of California decided, 6–1, that the death penalty violated the state's constitutional injunction, "nor shall cruel or unusual punishments be inflicted." Capital punishment, at least in California, offended "contemporary standards of decency." Infrequent executions—only two in the United States in 1967—suggested an arbitrary practice; and the length of time between sentence and execution amounted to "psychological torture." The state court bluntly concluded: "[C]apital punishment is impermissibly cruel. It degrades and dehumanizes all who participate in its processes. It is unnecessary to any legitimate goal of the state and is incompatible with the dignity of man and the judicial process."[13] Even though California voters quickly reversed the decision by constitutional initiative, the stage was set for a dramatic turn in judicial interpretation of cruel and unusual punishment.

The same year, 1972, in *Furman* v. *Georgia,* a 5–4 majority of the Supreme Court set aside the death penalty for three black defendants, two convicted of rape and one of murder. There was no majority opinion:

each of the five concurring justices reached the decision by separate routes. Only Marshall and Brennan concluded that the death penalty was cruel and unusual punishment within the meaning of the Eighth Amendment. By contemporary standards, each justice argued, capital punishment was inhumane, unnecessarily excessive, and morally unacceptable. Douglas, Stewart, and White objected on more limited grounds: the death penalty was arbitrary and capricious punishment; it discriminated against the poor, blacks, and other groups at the margins of society; and it failed to deter violent crime.

Chief Justice Burger, in dissent, protested that a majority of the Court did not hold the death penalty unconstitutional, but in effect the decision nullified the laws of thirty-nine states. It also forecast a new interpretation for the Eighth Amendment. All nine justices agreed that the death penalty was morally repugnant, and they concurred that, even though the framers of 1791 had not intended to abolish capital punishment, the amendment must be interpreted flexibly and in light of contemporary values. For executions to be constitutional, the Court implied, they must be administered consistently and fairly, without discriminatory intent or effect. Sentencing juries must be given objective standards to guide their choice of life or death. Above all, the punishment must be rational and reliable.[14]

Significantly, the decision reflected the influence of the Warren Court's result-oriented view of criminal justice. Punishment by death was qualitatively different from any other sanction: the penalty was unique; mistakes were irreversible. The decision to execute required not only strict adherence to objective and reliable rules but also strong assurance that it was proper in light of the crime, the defendant, and the patterns of punishment for similar crimes. At least in capital cases, equal justice joined fair procedure as a requirement of due process.

Guided by these standards, numerous states adopted mandatory death sentences for certain crimes, while other states established special post-trial hearings to determine whether to impose the death penalty. Reflecting a world-wide trend, states also reduced the number of capital crimes. The object of these reforms was to avoid arbitrary or capricious punishment; and in 1976, in *Gregg* v. *Georgia,* the Court, while declining to outlaw executions, accepted the two-stage process for capital cases, with guilt determined first and punishment fixed later.[15] But the same year and the next the Court refused to allow mandatory death sentences for the crimes of first-degree murder, rape, or killing of a police officer; and in 1978 the justices rejected an Ohio law that prescribed too narrowly the circumstances or conditions to be considered in condemning someone to death.[16] To pass constitutional muster, the justices seemed to conclude, courts must apply capital punishment equally yet fit the penalty to the circumstances of individual cases.

By the 1980s the inherent contradiction between equal justice and individual treatment became unacceptable to a majority of the justices. Although the Court intended the *Gregg* decision to make the process of punishment more rational—"No longer can a jury wantonly and freakishly impose the death sentence; it is always circumscribed by the legislative guidelines"[17]—the effect was to involve the Court ever more deeply in the supervision of capital convictions. Every inmate on death row sought a high court review, often repeatedly on different issues. Both state prosecutors and the general public viewed the years required to settle an appeal as a denial of justice, not a necessary delay to ensure fairness. Wearied by the issue, the Court retreated. Unable to accept the proposition that death was by definition cruel and unusual punishment, the justices abandoned the quest for reliability and settled instead for assurance that the process was not wholly arbitrary.

But by what standards would the justices determine arbitrariness? In a 1987 appeal, *McClesky* v. *Kemp,* opponents of the death penalty presented strong statistical evidence from 2,000 Georgia murder cases between 1973 and 1979 that race was significant in a jury's decision to impose capital punishment. Blacks convicted of killing whites were five times more likely to receive the death penalty than white murderers. The Court, now led by the conservative Chief Justice William Rehnquist, narrowly concluded that these figures made no difference. The decision reaffirmed a need for discretion in fitting the sentence to the circumstances of the crime. Racial bias may be a reason for setting aside a death sentence, but each defendant would have to prove that it affected his case.[18]

Appeals in capital cases commanded less of the Court's attention during the last half of the 1980s. And decisions in this area became decidedly more favorable to the state. In *Tison* v. *Arizona* (1987), for example, the justices accepted as constitutional statutes allowing capital punishment for anyone convicted of a felony in which a death occurred, whether or not they actually participated in the killing.[19] Satisfied that death was not cruel and unusual punishment and thus was constitutional, the Court retreated from further attempts to balance the competing goals of equal justice and individual treatment. One result was a steady increase in the number of executions. By 1990 there were over 2,700 inmates on death row, most of them black men. Yet there were few demands for the justices to reconsider their course. Indeed, public opinion polls throughout the 1980s demonstrated strong support for use of the death penalty as a deterrent to violent crime, even if empirical evidence failed to support this belief.

In other areas of criminal procedure, the Rehnquist Court generally declined to extend rights of the accused beyond the limits established in earlier cases. Law officers gained greater latitude in applying the *Miranda* rule when, in *Colorado* v. *Connelly* (1986), the justices adopted a less strict standard to determine whether or not a confession was truly voluntary. Police cannot fail to give the required *Miranda* warnings and must stop all questioning if a suspect demands a lawyer, but they can use nonthreatening tactics, such as pretending to sympathize with the suspect, to secure a valid confession.[20] Strengthening the ability of the police to fight crime was also the result in *United States* v. *Salerno* (1987), a decision that upheld the constitutionality of the Bail Reform Act of 1984 allowing the denial of bail if the government could demonstrate that releasing the person would endanger lives or safety. But even though an apparent departure from the presumption of innocence, the law itself provided numerous procedural safeguards to the defendant, including representation by counsel. These protections, the justices concluded, constituted a reasonable balance between the rights of the accused and the need for public security.[21]

One of the more interesting developments of the 1980s was the effort to re-establish state bills of rights as a primary guardian of individual rights. During most of American history, state courts had defined the terms of criminal due process, only to abandon this role in the 1950s and 1960s as the Warren Court created national standards of justice. But in an influential article published in 1977, Justice William Brennan, the dominant liberal on an increasingly conservative bench, reminded readers that the U. S. Supreme Court established only a floor for the protection of rights; the states can, if they choose, create broader guarantees.[22] Some state courts responded to this call. The Wisconsin court required that interpreters be provided at state expense for defendants who do not understand

English. The Michigan court concluded that a suspect should have an opportunity to request counsel at identification proceedings, a right not granted by the U. S. Supreme Court. In other instances—Mississippi, for example—the state's highest bench declined to accept the good faith exception to the exclusionary rule as part of state constitutional law.[23]

Yet there were reasons to doubt whether these cases represent a successful revival of the states' traditional role in maintaining the standards of criminal due process. State legislatures have passed tougher laws in response to increased public fear of crime; most of these statutes reject more expansive views of defendants' rights. Voters in numerous states have ratified amendments to their constitutions that deprive individuals of procedural rights they previously enjoyed. Connecticut in 1972 reduced the size of the criminal jury to as few as six persons in noncapital cases; Florida in 1982 retreated from a more liberal exclusionary rule to the one mandated by federal decisions; and numerous states now permit preventive detention, that is, holding suspects in custody for a period of time before charging them with crime.[24] This trend continued into the 1990s, in part because lawyers, most of them trained since 1960, have little experience in arguing state constitutional law. The constitutional tradition that flourished for over 150 years may have atrophied during the last several decades.

Epilogue

By the end of the 1980s rights of the accused were truly national, no longer dependent upon accidents of geography for their expression. Court decisions in large measure had redressed the imbalance of power that inevitably occurs in criminal proceedings when the state accuses an individual of wrongdoing. In restraining the hand of government, the Warren Court refused to heed ill-founded fears of disorder and honored instead the older American tradition of limiting power to promote liberty. The Court in the 1970s and 1980s did not abandon the new understanding of rights, despite widespread political demands to reverse the most controversial decisions. The justices concerned themselves more with finding the practical meaning of these safeguards in individual cases than with rejecting either in whole or in part the advances of earlier Courts.

The rights of defendants upon trial are not nearly so controversial today as are the pre-trial guarantees that restrain police practices. There remains a popular perception that the legal system protects criminal defendants at the expense of social order. It is difficult, at times, to rebut this conclusion. Too many crimes of violence crowd the headlines, too many drug-related crimes go unanswered, and too many people suffer innocently to dismiss easily the disorder that plagues modern America. What is much less certain is the relationship, if any, between crime and rights. Numerous studies continue to reveal that even the rulings most restrictive of police practices have only slight impact on the actual disposition of a case.

It is too early to know what modification or new interpretations the Supreme Court in the 1990s will make in the trial rights of defendants. Under the leadership of Chief Justice Rehnquist, who assumed his position in 1986, the Court has more often favored the prosecution than the defense. With the retirement of Justice Brennan, a law-and-order majority will likely control the Court for the next decade. But to date, the justices have not reversed completely the more liberal decisions of the Warren Court. One development worth watching is the re-emergence of state supreme courts as primary defenders of rights of the accused. The U. S. Supreme Court only establishes a minimum standard of conduct. Recently some state courts have begun to go beyond these national requirements. But many state supreme courts operate with elected judges, and voters may not support efforts to create more liberal trial rights.

It is inevitable that rights of the accused will acquire new interpretation in future years, although a return to earlier standards appears unlikely. These constitutional safeguards have indeed gained meaning from experience; undoubtedly, they will continue to do so. There will always exist fundamental differences on the proper balance between order and liberty, on the role of courts in establishing new rights, and on the definition of constitutional terms such as "equal protection" and "due process of law." What should be reassuring is the debate itself, which makes real the concept of popular democracy and revitalizes the American commitment to a society governed by law. But we cannot seek to restore the original expression of these rights, even if we could discern with certainty the framers' specific meaning. To do so would deny the potential of growth in our understanding of liberty, rights, and social responsibility. And it is this possibility that has kept the Bill of Rights a vital document a full two centuries after its adoption.

NOTES

Introduction

1. Steven Phillips. *No Heroes, No Villains: The Story of a Murder Trial* (New York, 1977). This book contains the story of the shooting and trial.

2. *Malinski* v. *New York*, 324 U.S. 401, 414 (1945).

3. *Shaughnessy* v. *United States*, 345 U.S. 206, 224 (1953).

4. Zechariah Chafee, Jr., *How Human Rights Got into the Constitution* (Boston, 1952), 44.

5. Joel P. Bishop, *Commentaries on the Criminal Law* (4th ed., Boston, 1868), xi.

6. Roscoe Pound, *Criminal Justice in America* (Providence, R.I., 1930), 57–58.

7. There are two legitimate parties in a criminal case—the state and the defendant(s). The victim and family or friends have an obvious interest, but in American law the state has the sole authority to prosecute. It does so on behalf of the victim and for the benefit of society at large.

8. David Fellman, *The Defendant's Rights Today* (Madison, Wisc., 1976), 11.

Chapter 1

1. William Bradford, *Of Plymouth Plantation,* ed., Samuel Eliot Morison (New York, 1963), 320–21.

2. The word inquest comes from the Latin *inquisito,* meaning inquisition, but it shares nothing in common with the canon law procedure used to identify and punish heretics against the church. Another name for the inquest was *recognitio,* or recognition, defined as a solemn answer or declaration of truth. Leonard W. Levy, *Origins of the Fifth Amendment: The Right Against Self-Incrimination* (New York, 1969), 7.

3. Levy, *Origins,* 17.

4. *Ibid.*, 29.

5. Sir John Fortescue, *De Laudibus Legum Angliae*, trans. by A. Amos (Cambridge, Eng., 1825), 93.

6. The quotation and much of the discussion of colonial law that follows is taken from Bradley Chapin, *Criminal Justice in Colonial America, 1606–1660* (Athens, Ga., 1983), 3 and *passim*.

7. Chapin, *Criminal Justice*, 4. In his study of early Massachusetts, David Konig notes that the "creation of legal institutions at the Bay Colony closely paralleled the suggestions and ideas put forth by the English reformers." David Thomas Konig, *Law and Society in Puritan Massachusetts: Essex County, 1629–1692* (Chapel Hill, N.C., 1979), 18.

8. Chapin, *Criminal Justice*, 5–8, 24 (quotation).

9. George Lee Haskins, *Law and Authority in Early Massachusetts; A Study in Tradition and Design* (New York, 1960), 196.

10. Bernard Schwartz, ed., *The Bill of Rights: A Documentary History* (2 vols., New York, 1971), I, 71–84.

11. The Pennsylvania, New Jersey, and New York documents are found in Schwartz, ed., *The Bill of Rights*, I, 126–44, 162–75, as are other documents mentioned in these pages.

12. Before the eighteenth century, there was little legal literature of any sort published in the colonies or referred to in law reports. Coke and Dalton not only were the standard works on English justice, often they were the only authors consulted. David Grayson Allen, *In English Ways: The Movement of Societies and the Transferral of English Local Law and Custom to Massachusetts Bay in the Seventeenth Century* (Chapel Hill, N.C., 1981), 209–10.

13. The list is from Chapin, *Criminal Justice*, 61.

14. Mark DeWolfe Howe, "The Sources and Nature of Law in Colonial Massachusetts," in George A. Billias, ed., *Law and Authority in Colonial America* (Barre, Mass., 1965), 1–16; Joseph H. Smith and Thomas G. Barnes, *The English Legal System: Carryover to the Colonies* (Los Angeles, 1975); Chapin, *Criminal Justice*, 4–15.

15. An excellent description of sixteenth-century English courtroom procedures can be found in John H. Langbein, "The Criminal Trial before the Lawyers," *Chicago Law Review*, 45 (Winter 1978), 263–316.

16. Quoted in Gail Sussman Marcus, " 'Due Execution of the Generall Rules of Righteousnesse': Criminal Procedure in New Haven Town and Colony, 1638–1658," in David D. Hall, John M. Murrin, and Thad W. Tate, eds., *Saint and Revolutionaries: Essays in Early American History* (New York, 1984), 101, hereafter referred to as "Criminal Procedure in New Haven."

17. Descriptions of New England trial procedures and much of the informa-

tion below can be found in Haskins, *Law and Authority in Early Massachusetts,* 196–212, and Marcus, "Criminal Procedure in New Haven."

18. An oath was a sacred pledge, and its use placed a suspect in the painful dilemma of risking eternal damnation with a false denial or of confirming the accusation and incriminating himself. Puritans vigorously opposed the use of oaths to compel self-incrimination, although some leaders, such as John Winthrop, would allow oaths where suspicions were strong. Haskins, *Law and Authority in Early Massachusetts,* 200–202. Also, see generally Levy, *Origins of the Fifth Amendment.*

19. This discussion owes much to John W. Murrin, "Magistrates, Sinners, and Precarious Liberty: Trial by Jury in Seventeenth-Century New England," in Hall, et al, eds., *Saints and Revolutionaries,* 152–206.

20. Even though more simple in structure, the court system in Virginia was not without its complexities. A full description of criminal jurisdictions of Virginia courts may be found in Peter H. Hoffer and William B. Scott, eds., *Criminal Proceedings in Colonial Virginia: The Richmond County Record of Finds, Examinations and Trials of Slaves, 1711–1754,* American Legal Records Series, Volume 10 (Washington, D.C., 1986). Also, see Hugh F. Rankin, *Criminal Trial Proceedings in the General Court of Colonial Virginia* (Charlottesville, Va., 1965).

21. Warren M. Billings, "Pleading, Procedure, and Practice: The Meaning of Due Process of Law in Seventeenth-Century Virginia," *Journal of Southern History,* 47 (November 1981), 569–84.

22. Philip J. Schwarz, "Forging the Shackles: The Development of Virginia's Criminal Code for Slaves," in David J. Bodenhamer and James W. Ely, Jr., eds., *Ambivalent Legacy: A Legal History of the South* (Jackson, Miss., 1984), 125–46.

23. A. G. Roeber, *Faithful Magistrates and Republican Lawyers: Creators of Virginia Legal Culture, 1680–1810* (Chapel Hill, N.C., 1981).

24. *National Mutual Insurance Co.* v. *Tidewater Transfer Co., Inc.,* 337 U.S. 582 (1948) at 646.

Chapter 2

1. Alexis de Tocqueville, *Notebooks,* ed. J. P. Mayer, trans. by George Lawrence as *Journey to America* (New York, 1971), 38.

2. J. G. A. Pocock, *The Ancient Constitution and the Feudal Law* (Cambridge, Eng., 1957), 30–69; Gordon S. Wood, *The Creation of the American Republic, 1776–1787* (Chapel Hill, N.C., 1969), 3–45.

3. John Phillip Reid, *Constitutional History of the American Revolution: The*

Authority of Rights (Madison, Wisc., 1986), 65–73, 109–11; Morton White, *The Philosophy of the American Revolution* (New York, 1978), 185–228.

4. Reid, *Constitutional History*, 73; Hendrik B. Hartog, "Losing the World of the Massachusetts Whig," in Hendrik B. Hartog, ed., *Law and the American Revolution* (New York, 1981).

5. Bernard Bailyn, *The Ideological Origins of the American Revolution* (Cambridge, Mass., 1967); Jack P. Greene, "From the Perspective of Law: Context and Legitimacy in the Origin of the American Revolution," *South Atlantic Quarterly*, 85 (1986), 56–77.

6. Reid, *Constitutional History*, 47–59.

7. William E. Nelson, "The Legal Restraint of Power in Pre-Revolutionary America: Massachusetts as a Case Study, 1760–1775," *American Journal of Legal History*, 18 (Jan., 1974), 1–32. The emerging emphasis on democracy and localism is discussed in Reid, *Constitutional History*, 49–51.

8. Edmund S. Morgan and Helen M. Morgan, *The Stamp Act Crisis: Prelude to Revolution* (Chapel Hill, N.C., 1953). The quotes are from Reid, *Constitutional History*, 177, 180.

9. David Ammerman, *In the Common Cause: American Response to the Coercive Acts of 1774* (Charlottesville, Va., 1974), 8–9. The Declaration and Resolves may be found in Bernard Schwartz, ed., *The Bill of Rights: A Documentary History* (2 vols., New York, 1971), I, 217.

10. Reid, *Constitutional History*, 169–70.

11. M. H. Smith, *The Writs of Assistance Case* (Berkeley, Cal., 1978).

12. Jacob W. Landynski, *Search and Seizure and the Supreme Court: A Study in Constitutional Interpretation* (Baltimore, 1966), 19–48, 39 (quotation).

13. Quoted in Landynski, *Search and Seizure and the Supreme Court*, 26.

14. Sir Matthew Hale, *The History of Pleas of the Crown* (2 vols., 1847), I. 474 *passim;* II, 105, 149–52.

15. Quoted in Landynski, *Search and Seizure and the Supreme Court*, 25.

16. *Ibid.*, 28–29.

17. L. K. Wroth and Hiller B. Zoebel, eds., *The Legal Papers of John Adams* (3 vols., Cambridge, Mass., 1965), II, 123–30, 134–44.

18. Reid, *Constitutional History*, 197–98.

19. William Cuddihy and B. Carmon Hardy, "A Man's House Was Not His Castle: Origins of the Fourth Amendment to the United States Constitution," *William and Mary Quarterly*, 3rd Series, 37 (1980), 371–400.

20. "Address to the Inhabitants of Quebec," in Schwartz, ed., *The Bill of Rights: A Documentary History*, I, 222–23.

21. "Virginia Declaration of Rights," in Schwartz, ed., *The Bill of Rights: A Documentary History*, I, 234–36.

22. The New Jersey, Pennsylvania, and Georgia documents are found in

Schwartz, ed., *The Bill of Rights: A Documentary History*, I, 256–61 (New Jersey), 263–75 (Pennsylvania), 291–300 (Georgia).

23. William M. Beaney, *Right to Counsel in American Courts* (Ann Arbor, Mich., 1955), 8–24.

24. "Candid and Critical Remarks on a Letter Signed Ludlow," in Philip S. Foner, ed., *The Complete Works of Thomas Paine* (New York, 1961 repr. of 1945 edition), 273–74.

25. Sir William Blackstone, *Commentaries on the Laws of England, Book the Fourth* (4 vols., New York, 1969 repr. of 1803 edition); Lawrence M. Friedman, *A History of American Law* (New York, 1973), 88–90.

26. See, in general, Wood, *Creation of the American Republic*.

27. Bernard Bailyn, "Political Experience and Enlightenment Ideas in Eighteenth Century America," *American Historical Review*, 67 (Jan., 1962), 339–51; Peter Charles Hoffer, *Revolution and Regeneration: Life Cycle and the Historical Vision of the Generation of 1776* (Athens, Ga., 1983), 14–69.

28. Samuel Walker, *Popular Justice: A History of American Criminal Justice* (New York, 1980), 35–40.

29. Cesare Beccaria, *On Crimes and Punishments*, trans. Henry Paolucci (Indianapolis, 1963); Marcello T. Maestro, *Cesare Beccaria and the Origins of Penal Reform* (Philadelphia, 1973), 12–33.

30. David J. Rothman, *Discovery of the Asylum: Social Order and Disorder in the New Republic* (Boston, 1971), 56–58.

31. "Massachusetts Declaration of Rights," in Schwartz, ed., *The Bill of Rights: A Documentary History*, I, 339–44.

32. Excellent treatments of the post-Constitutional Convention development of the Bill of Rights may be found in Robert Allen Rutland, *The Birth of the Bill of Rights* (Chapel Hill, N.C., 1963), 126–218; Bernard Schwartz, *The Great Rights of Mankind: A History of the American Bill of Rights* (New York, 1977), 92–191.

33. Edmund S. Morgan, *Inventing the People: The Rise of Popular Sovereignty in England and America* (New York, 1988).

34. "The Address and Reasons of Dissent of the Minority of the Convention of the State of Pennsylvania to Their Constituents," in Schwartz, ed., *The Bill of Rights: A Documentary History*, II, 667.

35. *Ibid.*, 668.

36. Kenneth R. Bowling, " 'A Tub to the Whale': The Founding Fathers and Adoption of the Federal Bill of Rights," *Journal of the Early Republic*, 8 (Fall 1988), 223–52; Julius Goebel, Jr., *History of the Supreme Court of the United States: Antecedents and Beginnings to 1801* (New York, 1971), Chap. 10.

37. Rutland, *Birth of the Bill of Rights*, 218.

Chapter 3

1. Leon Radzinowicz, *Ideology and Crime* (New York, 1965), 25.

2. *Barron* v. *Baltimore,* 7 Peters 243 (1833); *U.S.* v. *Hudson and Goodwin,* 7 Cranch 32 (1812).

3. *Annals of Congress,* I, 430, as cited in Bernard Schwartz, ed., *The Bill of Rights: A Documentary History* (2 vols., New York, 1971), II, 1031.

4. Morton J. Horwitz, *The Transformation of American Law, 1780–1860* (Cambridge, Mass., 1977), 1–30.

5. Horwitz, *Transformation of American Law,* 11, 16–17.

6. Joseph Chitty, *A Practical Treatise on Criminal Law* (2 vols., Boston, 1837), I, 237.

7. David J. Bodenhamer, *The Pursuit of Justice: Crime and Law in Antebellum Indiana* (New York, 1986), 33–34.

8. Bodenhamer, *Pursuit of Justice,* 34–36.

9. *Leach's Crown Cases* 263 (1783).

10. Justine Tharp Tilger, "The Nineteenth Century Background of the *Escobeda* and *Miranda* Rules (doctoral dissertation, Indiana University, 1971), 60–64.

11. Bodenhamer, *Pursuit of Justice,* 36–40.

12. Leonard W. Levy, *The Law of the Commonwealth and Chief Justice Shaw: The Evolution of American Law, 1830–1860* (Cambridge, Mass., 1957), 282–89; *Fisher* v. *McGirr,* 1 Gray (Mass.), 33, 40–41.

13. William E. Nelson, *Americanization of the Common Law: The Impact of Legal Change on Massachusetts Society, 1760–1820* (Cambridge, Mass., 1975), 89–144.

14. Cesare Beccaria, *On Crimes and Punishments,* trans. Henry Paolucci (Indianapolis, 1963), 43–44.

15. David Brion Davis, "The Movement to Abolish Capital Punishment in America, 1787–1861," *American Historical Review,* 63 (Oct. 1957), 28–42.

16. The Rush and Hamilton quotations are found in Louis P. Masur, *Rites of Execution: Capital Punishment and the Transformation of American Culture, 1776–1865* (New York, 1989), 65, 85.

17. *Ibid.*

18. William Bradford, *An Enquiry How Far the Punishment of Death Is Necessary in Pennsylvania* (Philadelphia, 1793), repr. in *American Journal of Legal History,* 12 (1968), 122–75, 245–70.

19. David J. Rothman, *The Discovery of the Asylum: Social Order and Disorder in the New Republic* (Boston, 1971), 61.

20. As quoted in Eli Faber, "Restraining the Death Penalty: The Era of the Founding Fathers." Paper presented at the annual meeting of Society for the Historians of the Early Republic, Knoxville, Tennessee, July 1986.

21. Bodenhamer, *Pursuit of Justice*, 14–17.

22. Davis, "The Movement to Abolish Capital Punishment."

23. Richard D. Younger, *The People's Panel: The Grand Jury in the United States, 1634–1941* (Providence, R.I., 1963), 57–84.

24. David J. Bodenhamer, "Criminal Justice and Democratic Theory in Antebellum America: The Grand Jury Debate in Indiana," *Journal of the Early Republic,* 5 (Winter 1985), 281–302.

25. Note, "The Changing Role of the Jury in the Nineteenth Century," *Yale Law Review,* 74 (Nov. 1964), 170; David J. Bodenhamer, "The Democratic Impulse and Legal Change in the Age of Jackson: The Example of Criminal Juries in Antebellum Indiana," *The Historian,* 45 (Feb. 1983), 206–19.

26. Lawrence M. Friedman, *A History of American Law* (New York, 1973), 248–64.

27. Robert Fogelson, *Big City Police* (Cambridge, Mass., 1977); Samuel Walker, *A Critical History of Police Reform: The Emergence of Professionalism* (Lexington, Mass., 1977).

28. Bodenhamer, *Pursuit of Justice,* 99–110.

29. *Ibid.,* 96–99; Allen Steinberg, *The Transformation of Criminal Justice: Philadelphia, 1800–1880* (Chapel Hill, N.C., 1989).

30. Kathryn Preyer, "Crime, the Criminal Law, and Reform in Post-Revolutionary Virginia," *Law and History Review,* 1 (1985), 53–85. Michael Stephen Hindus, *Prison and Plantation: Crime, Justice, and Authority in Massachusetts and South Carolina, 1767–1878* (Chapel Hill, N.C., 1980), 57–124.

31. Elizabeth Gaspar Brown, "Judge James Doty's Notes of Trials and Opinions: 1823–1832," *American Journal of Legal History,* 9 (1965), 17–40, 156–66, 216–33, 350–62.

32. Philip J. Schwarz, "Forging the Shackles: The Development of Virginia's Criminal Code for Slaves," in David J. Bodenhamer and James W. Ely, Jr., eds., *Ambivalent Legacy: A Legal History of the South* (Jackson, Miss., 1984), 125–46.

33. As quoted in Kermit L. Hall, *The Magic Mirror: Law in American History* (New York, 1989), 133.

34. Daniel Flanigan, "Criminal Procedure in Slave Trials in the Antebellum South," *Journal of Southern History,* 40 (Aug. 1974), 537–64.

35. Hall, *The Magic Mirror,* 175–76.

Chapter 4

1. *McCorkle* v. *State*, 14 Ind. 41 (1859); Indianapolis *Daily Indiana Journal*, March 19, 1860.

2. Charles Loring Brace, *The Dangerous Classes of New York and Twenty Years Work Among Them* (New York, 1872), 28–29.

3. Loren P. Beth, *The Development of the American Constitution, 1877–1917* (New York, 1971), 201–203.

4. William F. Dukes, *A Constitutional History of Habeas Corpus* (Westport, Conn., 1980).

5. *Ex Parte Merryman*, Fed. Cases No. 9487 (1861): 312.

6. Harold Hyman and William C. Wiecek, *Equal Justice Under Law: Constitutional Development, 1835–1875* (New York, 1982), 240–41.

7. *Ibid.*, 260–61.

8. Mark deWolfe Howe, "Federalism and Civil Rights," Massachusetts Historical Society *Proceedings*, LXX (1965), 24–25.

9. Herman Belz, *Emancipation and Equal Rights* (New York, 1978), 108–40.

10. Beth, *Development of the American Constitution*, 191–215.

11. Belz, *Emancipation and Civil Rights*, xiii.

12. *Hurtado* v. *California*, 110 U.S. 516 (1884).

13. *Slaughterhouse Cases*, 16 Wallace 36 (1873), 365.

14. Beth, *Development of the American Constitution*, 200–203.

15. G. Edward White, *The American Judicial Tradition: Profiles of Leading American Judges* (New York, 1977), 84–108.

16. William C. Wiecek, *Liberty Under Law: The Supreme Court in American Life* (Baltimore, 1988), 110–20.

17. *Abel* v. *United States*, 362 U.S. 217, 255 (1960), dissenting opinion.

18. Jacob W. Landynski, *Search and Seizure and the Supreme Court: A Study in Constitutional Interpretation* (Baltimore, 1966), 49–50.

19. *Murray* v. *Hoboken Land Co.*, 18 Howard 272 (1855).

20. *Boyd* v. *United States*, 116 U.S. 616, 632 (1886).

21. *Weeks* v. *United States*, 232 U.S. 383, 393 (1914).

22. Landynski, *Search and Seizure*, 62–86.

23. *Carroll* v. *United States*, 267 U.S. 132, 153–54 (1925).

24. *Olmstead* v. *United States*, 277 U.S. 438, 464, 470–85 (1928).

25. Richard C. Cortner, *The Supreme Court and the Second Bill of Rights: The Fourteenth Amendment and the Nationalization of Civil Liberties* (Madison, Wisc., 1981), 12–24.

26. *Davidson* v. *New Orleans*, 96 U.S. 97, 103 (1878).

27. *Hurtado* v. *California*, 530, 534–38.

28. *Ibid.*, 541.

29. Cortner, *Supreme Court and the Second Bill of Rights*, 22–24.

30. *Twining* v. *New Jersey*, 211 U.S. 78, 105 (1908).

31. Cortner, *Supreme Court and the Second Bill of Rights*, 38–50.

32. Herbert A. Johnson, *History of Criminal Justice* (Columbus, Ohio, 1988), 217–33.

33. Samuel Walker, *Popular Justice: A History of American Criminal Justice* (New York, 1980), 108–44.

34. Kermit L. Hall, *The Magic Mirror: Law in American History* (New York, 1989), 178–88.

35. Milton Heumann, "A Note on Plea Bargaining and Case Pressure," *Law and Society Review*, 9 (1975), 515–28.

36. Albert W. Alschuler, "Plea Bargaining and Its History," *Columbia Law Review*, 79 (Jan. 1979), 1–43.

37. Susan C. Towne, "The Historical Origins of Bench Trial for Serious Crimes," *American Journal of Legal History*, 16 (1982), 123–59.

38. Alschuler, "Plea Bargaining and Its History," 19–24.

39. *Ibid.*, 26.

40. *Ibid.*, 30.

41. Lawrence M. Friedman and Robert V. Percival, *The Roots of Justice: Crime and Punishment in Alameda County, California, 1870–1910* (Chapel Hill, N.C., 1981), 237–60.

42. *Ibid.*, 135–95.

43. *Ibid.*, 67–134.

44. Beth, *Development of the American Constitution*, 235.

45. Neil R. McMillen, *Dark Journey: Black Mississippians in the Age of Jim Crow* (Urbana, Ill., 1989), 197–223.

46. *Ibid.*

47. *Ibid.*

48. *Ibid.*

Chapter 5

1. Dan T. Carter, *Scottsboro: A Tragedy of the American South* (rev. ed., Baton Rouge, La., 1979), 3–10.

2. *Ibid.*, 11–50.

3. *Powell* v. *Alabama*, 287 U.S. 45, 46, 72–77 (1932).

4. Grant Gilmore, *The Ages of American Law* (New Haven, Conn., 1977), Chap. 4.

5. Robert K. Murray, *Red Scare: A Study in National Hysteria, 1919–1920* (New York, 1955).

6. John W. Johnson, *American Legal Culture, 1908–1940* (Westport, Conn., 1981), 58–60.

7. William M. Tuttle, Jr., *Race Riot: Chicago in the Red Summer of 1919* (New York, 1970), 32–66; Samuel Walker, *Popular Justice: A History of American Criminal Justice* (New York, 1980), 164–66.

8. Mary Frances Berry and John W. Blassingame, *Long Memory: The Black Experience in America* (New York, 1982), 123.

9. National Commission on Law Observance and Enforcement, *Lawlessness in Law Enforcement* (Washington, 1931).

10. Paul L. Murphy, *The Constitution in Crisis Times, 1918–1969* (New York, 1972), 68–71.

11. *Brown* v. *Mississippi,* 297 U.S. 278, 285–86 (1936).

12. *Palko* v. *Connecticut,* 302 U.S. 319, 325–26 (1937).

13. *Ibid.,* 325–28.

14. *Ibid.*

15. Gerald T. Dunne, *Hugo Black and the Judicial Revolution* (New York, 1977), Chap. 12.

16. Richard C. Cortner, *The Supreme Court and the Second Bill of Rights: The Fourteenth Amendment and the Nationalization of Civil Liberties* (Madison, Wisc., 1981), Chaps. 6 and 7.

17. *Malinski* v. *New York,* 324 U.S. 405, 414–15 (1945).

18. William M. Wiecek, *Liberty under Law: The Supreme Court in American Life* (Baltimore, 1988), 2–4.

19. *McNabb* v. *United States,* 318 U.S. 332, 347 (1943).

20. *Chambers* v. *Florida,* 309 U.S. 227, 236 (1940).

21. *Johnson* v. *Zerbst,* 304 U.S. 458 (1938).

22. *Betts* v. *Brady,* 316 U.S. 455, 471 (1942).

23. *Foster* v. *Illinois,* 332 U.S. 134, 138–39 (1947).

24. *Bute* v. *Illinois,* 333 U.S. 640, 677 (1948).

25. *Screws* v. *United States,* 325 U.S. 91 (1945).

26. *Adamson* v. *California,* 332 U.S. 46 (1947).

27. *In re Oliver,* 333 U.S. 257 (1948); Cortner, *The Supreme Court and the Second Bill of Rights,* 152–61.

28. *Wolf* v. *Colorado,* 338 U.S. 25, 27–28 (1949).

29. Jacob W. Landynski, *Search and Seizure and the Supreme Court: A Study in Constitutional Interpretation* (Baltimore, 1966), 127–34.

30. *Wolf* v. *Colorado,* 46–48.

31. *Rochin* v. *California,* 342 U.S. 165, 172–73.

32. *Irvine* v. *California,* 348 U.S. 128 (1954).

33. *Breithaupt* v. *Abram,* 352 U.S. 432 (1957).

34. *Ibid.,* 442.

35. Justice Brennan, quoted in Cortner, *The Supreme Court and the Second Bill of Rights*, 173.

36. *Rochin* v. *California*, 170.

37. Cortner, *The Supreme Court and the Second Bill of Rights*, Chap. 7.

Chapter 6

1. G. Edward White, *Earl Warren: A Public Life* (New York, 1982), Chap. 15.

2. G. Edward White, *Patterns of American Legal Thought* (New York, 1978).

3. Earl Warren, *The Memoirs of Earl Warren* (1977), 332–33, as quoted in White, *Earl Warren*, 220.

4. White, *Earl Warren*, Chap. 9.

5. Earl Warren, ''The Law and the Future,'' *Fortune* (November 1955), 106, 226.

6. Alfred H. Kelley, Winfred Harbison, and Herman Belz, *The American Constitutional Tradition: Origins and Development* (6th ed., New York, 1983), 635–37.

7. Jacob W. Landynski, *Search and Seizure in the Supreme Court: A Study in Constitutional Interpretation* (Baltimore, 1966), 144.

8. *Rea* v. *United States*, 350 U.S. 214, 217 (1956).

9. *Elkins* v. *United States*, 364 U.S. 206, 221, 223 (1960).

10. Richard C. Cortner, *The Supreme Court and the Second Bill of Rights: The Fourteenth Amendment and the Nationalization of Civil Liberties* (Madison, Wisc., 1981), 179–81.

11. *Mapp* v. *Ohio*, 367 U.S. 643, 656, 658 (1961).

12. *Ibid.*, 673.

13. Cortner, *The Supreme Court and the Second Bill of Rights*, 181–84.

14. *Robinson* v. *California*, 370 U.S. 660, 667 (1962).

15. Anthony Lewis, ''A Talk with Warren on Crime, the Court, and the Country,'' *New York Times Magazine* (Oct. 19, 1969), 124.

16. Anthony Lewis, *Gideon's Trumpet* (New York, 1964).

17. *Gideon* v. *Wainwright*, 372 U.S. 335, 344 (1963).

18. As quoted in Cortner, *The Supreme Court and the Second Bill of Rights*, 196.

19. *Malloy* v. *Hogan*, 378 U.S. 1 (1964).

20. *Ibid.*, 11.

21. *Ibid.*, 15, 32–33.

22. *Pointer* v. *Texas*, 380 U.S. 400, 405 (1965).

23. As quoted in Cortner, *The Supreme Court and the Second Bill of Rights*, 222.

24. *Pointer* v. *Texas*, 380 U.S. 410–14.

25. Cortner, *The Supreme Court and the Second Bill of Rights*, 292–93.

26. *Ibid.*, 294–98.

27. *Spano* v. *New York*, 360 U.S. 315 (1959); *Escobedo* v. *Illinois*, 378 U.S. 478 (1964).

28. *Miranda* v. *Arizona*, 384 U.S. 457 (1966).

29. *Ibid.*, 470–75.

30. Lewis, "A Talk with Warren," 126.

31. *Miranda* v. *Arizona*, 572.

32. Samuel Walker, *Popular Justice: A History of American Criminal Justice* (New York, 1980), 231–32.

33. *Ibid.*

34. White, *Earl Warren*, 271.

35. *Ibid.*, 272–75.

36. Paul Murphy, *The Constitution in Crisis Times, 1918–1969* (New York, 1972), 430–31.

37. *In re Gault*, 387 U.S. 1 (1967).

38. Murphy, *Constitution in Crisis Times*, 432–33.

39. *Washington* v. *Texas*, 388 U.S. 14 (1967).

40. *Klopfer* v. *North Carolina*, 386 U.S. 213 (1967).

41. *Duncan* v. *Louisiana*, 391 U.S. 145 (1968).

42. *Ibid.*, 150.

43. Murphy, *Constitution in Crisis Times*, 433–34.

44. *Katz* v. *United States*, 389 U.S. 347, 354 (1967).

45. Murphy, *Constitution in Crisis Times*, 437–38.

46. *Ibid.*, 439.

47. *Benton* v. *Maryland*, 395 U.S. 784, 790–95 (1969).

Chapter 7

1. *Frazier* v. *United States*, 419 F. 2d 1161, 1176 (1969), as quoted in Leonard W. Levy, *Against the Law: The Nixon Court and Criminal Justice* (New York, 1976), 17.

2. Earl Warren, "The Law and the Future," *Fortune* (November 1955), 106, 226.

3. *New York Times*, July 4, 1971, 1, 24.

4. *United States* v. *Harris*, 403 U.S. 573, 582 (1971).

5. Alfred H. Kelly, Winfred A. Harbison, and Herman Belz, *The American Constitution: Its Origins and Development* (6th ed., 1983), 718–19.

6. *United States* v. *Calandra*, 414 U.S. 338, 348, 354 (1974).

7. *United States* v. *Leon*, 468 U.S. 897 (1984); Yale Kamisar, "The 'Police

Practice' Phases of the Criminal Process and the Three Phases of the Burger Court,'' in Herman Schwartz, ed., *The Burger Years: Rights and Wrongs in the Supreme Court, 1969–1986* (New York, 1987), 164–66.

8. Melvin I. Urofsky, *A March of Liberty: A Constitutional History of the United States* (New York, 1988), 932.

9. Kelly, et al, *The American Constitution*, 719; *Illinois* v. *Gates*, 462 U.S. 213, 244 (1983), quotation.

10. Kelly, et al, *The American Constitution*, 720; Stephen A. Saltzburg, "Foreword: The Flow and Ebb of Constitutional Criminal Procedure in the Warren and Burger Courts,'' *Georgetown Law Journal*, 69 (1980), 488.

11. Michael Meltsner, *Cruel and Unusual: The Supreme Court and Capital Punishment* (New York, 1973); Peter Passell, "The Deterrent Effect of the Death Penalty: A Statistical Test,'' *Stanford Law Review*, 28 (Nov. 1975), 61–80.

12. David Fellman, *The Defendant's Rights Today* (Madison, Wisc., 1975), 388–89.

13. *Ibid.*, 390.

14. *Furman* v. *Georgia*, 408 U.S. 238 (1972).

15. *Gregg* v. *Georgia*, 428 U.S. 153 (1976).

16. *Woodson* v. *North Carolina*, 428 U.S. 280 (1976); *Roberts* v. *Louisiana*, 431 U.S. 633 (1977); *Lockett* v. *Ohio*, 438 U.S. 586 (1978).

17. *Gregg* v. *Georgia*, 206–207.

18. *McClesky* v. *Kemp*, 481 U.S. 279 (1987). This discussion of Rehnquist Court decisions owes much to Urofsky, *A March of Liberty*, 957–69.

19. *Tison* v. *Arizona*, 481 U.S. 137 (1987).

20. *Colorado* v. *Connelly*, 479 U.S. 157 (1986). Four years later, the Court declined, 6–2, to weaken *Miranda* further when it held that once the suspect requested counsel, all questioning must stop until a lawyer was present, whether or not the accused has consulted with an attorney. *Minnick* v. *Mississippi*, 59 L.W. 4037 (1990).

21. *United States* v. *Salerno*, 481 U.S. 739 (1987).

22. William J. Brennan, Jr., "State Constitutions and the Protection of Individual Rights,'' *Harvard Law Review*, 90 (1977), 489–504.

23. Shirley S. Abrahamson, "Criminal Law and State Constitutions: The Emergence of State Constitutional Law,'' *Texas Law Review*, 63 (1985), 1141–94.

24. Donald E. Wilkes, Jr., "First Things Last: Amendomania and State Bills of Rights,'' *Mississippi Law Journal*, 54 (1984), 223–59.

SUGGESTIONS FOR FURTHER READING

The secondary literature on rights of the accused is rich but unbalanced. Scholars have written in abundance on twentieth-century developments, especially as revealed in modern case law; by comparison, they have scarcely addressed the eighteenth and nineteenth centuries. Except for this book, there is no comprehensive historical survey of these protections. Such gaps in treatment suggest, incorrectly, that the rights found in the Fourth, Fifth, Sixth, and Eighth Amendments were stepchildren within the Bill of Rights, at least until the Supreme Court in the 1960s restored them to full equality with their more illustrious siblings, the First Amendment's guarantees of free speech, press, religion, and assembly. Although this book sketches the evolution of defendants' rights under state protection, readers in search of information about the pre-modern period must continue to examine a wide variety of sources.

General Works

Understanding the rights of the accused must occur within the broader framework of Anglo-American constitutional history. The standard text here is Alfred Kelley, Winfred Harbison, and Herman Belz, *The American Constitution; Its Origin and Development* (6th ed., 1983), prized for its ability to relate public law to political and social developments. Mel Urofsky, *A March of Liberty: A Constitutional History of the United States* (1988), is equally masterful, while devoting somewhat more attention to rights of the accused. Special focus on the Bill of Rights, including the publication of important documents and an accessible commentary, may be found in Bernard Schwartz, ed., *The Bill of Rights: A Documentary History* (2 vols., 1971). Summary information on particular cases or legal concepts is in Kermit L. Hall, James W. Ely, Jr., William Wiecek, and Joel Grossman, eds., *The Oxford Companion to the Supreme Court* (1991).

American legal history, a field that includes both public and private law, is the subject of a pioneering work by Lawrence M. Friedman, *A History of American Law* (2nd ed., 1985). Although skimpy on the twentieth century, Friedman devotes considerable attention to criminal justice and the rights of the accused. Much fuller on modern developments and more comprehensive on nineteenth-century criminal justice is Kermit L. Hall, *The Magic Mirror: Law in American History* (1988). Both Friedman and Hall recognize the role of state courts in shaping American constitutional law, a result overlooked in many texts that focus on the U. S. Supreme Court. Hall's work contains an especially good bibliography. Also worthy of mention are two compilations of essays: *Criminal Procedure*, Vol. 7, in Paul L. Murphy, ed., *The Bill of Rights and American Legal History* (9 vols., 1990), and *Crime and Criminal Law*, Vol. 13, in Kermit L. Hall, ed., *United States Constitutional and Legal History* (20 vols., 1987). Both collections reprint articles from journals not generally available in undergraduate and public libraries.

In addition to constitutional history, readers interested in the rights of the accused should consult works on criminal justice. The most useful and readable general treatment is Samuel Walker, *Popular Justice: A History of American Criminal Justice* (1980). Herbert A. Johnson, *History of Criminal Justice*, surveys developments since the ancient world and necessarily treats the American experience in briefer compass, yet he offers a satisfactory overview. *Courts and Criminal Procedure*, Vol. 2, in Eric Monkkonen, ed., *Crime and Justice in American History* (16 vols., 1990), contains numerous articles of value. An older but still useful work is Roscoe Pound, *Criminal Justice in America* (1930).

Chapter 1—The Colonial Background

The 1960s and 1970s witnessed an explosion of scholarship on the American colonies, especially on the social and legal worlds of the early settlers. Although New England was the focus of much of this work, there now exists sufficient study of the other colonies to justify generalizations about rights of the accused in the decades preceding the American Revolution. Bradley Chapin, *Criminal Justice in Colonial America, 1606–1660* (1983), traces the comparative development of the early colonial codes. No similar treatment exists for the late seventeenth and eighteenth centuries. Legal historian Leonard W. Levy's definitive work, *Origins of the Fifth Amendment: The Right Against Self-Incrimination* (1969), discusses both the English and colonial background of this important right of the accused.

There are several model studies on individual colonies, although none discuss criminal law exclusively. Among the best is David T. Konig, *Law and Society in Puritan Massachusetts, Essex County, 1629–1692* (1979). Also worthy of note are two other studies of the Bay Colony: George L. Haskins, *Law and Authority in Early Massachusetts: A Study in Tradition and Design* (1960), and David Grayson Allen, *In English Ways: The Movement of Societies and the Transferral of English Local Law and Custom to Massachusetts Bay in the Seventeenth Century* (1981). Other colonies have received less attention from historians. Julius Goebel, Jr., and T. Raymond Naughton, *Law Enforcement in Colonial New York: A Study in Criminal Procedure, 1664–1776* (1970), offer an extraordinarily detailed look at the colony's criminal process, but the treatment suffers from its overly technical focus. More enlightening for the general reader is Douglas Greenberg, *Crime and Law Enforcement in the Colony of New York* (1976). An early study of Virginia is Arthur P. Scott, *Criminal Law in Colonial Virginia* (1930). Colonial North Carolina receives attention in Donna J. Spindel, *Crime and Society in North Carolina, 1663–1776* (1989).

Articles and essays contain much valuable information about rights of the accused during the colonial period. An excellent description of sixteenth-century English courtroom practice, also applicable in large measure to the colonies, is found in John H. Langbein, "The Criminal Trial before the Lawyers," *Chicago Law Review* (1978). For an understanding of how much the colonists modified English practice, see Warren Billings, "Pleading, Procedure, and Practice: The Meaning of Due Process of Law in Seventeenth-Century Virginia," *Journal of Southern History* (1981), a work that should be compared with David T. Konig, "'Dale's Laws' and the Non-Common Law Origins of Criminal Justice in Virginia," *American Journal of Legal History* (1982). The influence of religious belief on criminal procedure is discussed in two essays in David D. Hall, John Murrin, and Thad W. Tate, eds., *Saints and Revolutionaries: Essays in Early American History* (1984): Gail Sussman Marcus, "'Due Execution of the Generall Rules of Righteousnesse'; Criminal Procedure in New Haven Town and Colony, 1683–1658"; and John W. Murrin, "Magistrates, Sinners, and Precarious Liberty: Trial by Jury in Seventeenth-Century New England." Kathryn Preyer surveys colonial criminal law in "Penal Measures in the American Colonies: An Overview," *American Journal of Legal History* (1982), while Peter Hoffer offers a suggestive interpretation of Virginia justice in "Disorder and Deference: The Paradoxes of Criminal Justice in the Colonial Tidewater," in David J. Bodenhamer and James W. Ely, Jr., eds., *Ambivalent Legacy: A Legal History of the South* (1984).

Much can be learned from published colonial court records, especially documents edited and introduced by legal historians. Among the most useful of these records are: Peter H. Hoffer and William B. Scott, eds., *Criminal Proceedings in Colonial Virginia: The Richmond County Record of Finds, Examinations, and Trials of Slaves, 1711–1754* (1986); Hugh F. Rankin, ed., *Criminal Trial Proceedings in the General Court of Colonial Virginia* (1965);

and Joseph H. Smith, ed., *Criminal Justice in Western Massachusetts (1639–1702): The Pynchon Court Record, an Original Judge's Diary of the Administration of Justice in the Springfield Court of Massachusetts Bay Colony* (1961).

Chapter 2—The Revolutionary Legacy

The American conception of rights may have roots in the colonial period, but it received nourishment and expression during the intellectual ferment of the Revolutionary years. Although subject to various meanings, republicanism is one key to understanding the debate with Great Britain and the subsequent establishment of independent government. Gordon Wood, *The Creation of the American Republic* (1969), remains the most complete introduction to republican ideas and values. But there was more than a single intellectual progenitor to the Revolution and Constitution, as Forrest McDonald brilliantly argues in *Novus Ordo Seclorum: The Intellectual Origins of the Constitution* (1985), undoubtedly the best treatment of the subject. In a series of books on the constitutional and legal history of the Revolution, John Phillip Reid convincingly relates the ideological currents of the period to colonial experiences under British imperial rule. Reid's *Constitutional History of the American Revolution: The Authority of Rights* (1986) is essential reading for understanding the rebels' insistence on the sanctity of their rights as Englishmen. Morton H. Smith provides an excellent study of the protections against search and seizure in *The Writs of Assistance Case* (1978), as does David Ammerman for several other guarantees in *In the Common Cause: American Response to the Coercive Acts of 1774* (1974).

There have been surprising few books written on the creation of the Bill of Rights, perhaps because the documentary record is so slim. Clearly the best treatment of the subject is Robert Allen Rutland, *The Birth of the Bill of Rights* (1963). Bernard Schwartz discusses the creation of the first ten amendments and surveys their subsequent history in *The Great Rights of Mankind: A History of the Bill of Rights* (1977). Another useful work is Irving Brant, *The Bill of Rights: Its Origin and Meaning* (1965). A good brief introduction is Kenneth R. Bowling, " 'A Tub to the Whale': The Founding Fathers and Adoption of the Federal Bill of Rights," *Journal of the Early Republic* (1988). Willi Paul Adams surveys the revolutionary state constitutions and their protection of rights in *The First American Constitutions: Republican Ideology and the Making of State Constitutions in the Revolutionary Era* (1980).

There is a larger literature on the rights contained in the Fourth, Fifth, Sixth, and Eighth Amendments, although much of it discusses subsequent case law rather than the history of the amendments or the rights they contain. In addition to Leonard Levy, *Origins of the Fifth Amendment* (1969), an exception to the post-adoption focus of most books, readers may wish to consult the following works:

Jacob W. Landynski, *Search and Seizure and the Supreme Court: A Study in Constitutional Interpretation* (1966); William M. Beany, *Right to Counsel in American Courts* (1955); Jay A. Sigler, *Double Jeopardy: The Development of a Legal and Social Policy* (1969). An important article is William B. Cuddihy and B. Carmon Hardy, "A Man's House Was Not His Castle: Origins of the Fourth Amendment to the United States Constitution," *William and Mary Quarterly* (1980). The impact of the Revolution on American law is explored in the essays in Hendrik B. Hartog, ed., *Law and The American Revolution and the Revolution in Law* (1981), while William E. Nelson, "Emerging Notions of Criminal Law in the Revolutionary Era: An Historical Perspective," *New York University Law Review* (1967) provides an excellent introduction to changes in criminal law.

Chapter 3—Due Process in the New Republic

There is no adequate single-volume introduction to rights of the accused during the nineteenth century. Most scholars have written as if these rights experienced little or no development from the time of their incorporation into the Constitution until the mid-twentieth century. The belief that criminal law was a matter for the states and the limited application of federal criminal law explains the oversight. Consequently, the student of these guarantees must examine a wide range of scholarly literature to discover the evolution of these rights, especially in the states. For federal law, readers should consult Dwight F. Henderson, *Congress, Courts, and Criminal: The Development of Federal Criminal Law, 1801–1829* (1985). Also valuable is a symposium issue of *Law and History Review* (1986), with articles by Kathryn Preyer and Robert C. Palmer on the common law of crimes in the early republic.

Several scholars have examined the various changes in American law, especially economic law, during the early national and antebellum decades. Morton J. Horowitz, *The Transformation of American Law, 1780–1860* (1977) and William E. Nelson, *The Americanization of the Common Law: The Impact of Legal Change on Massachusetts Society, 1760–1820* (1975) are the best guides to these changes, although historians debate whether the experience of other states paralleled that of Massachusetts. In *The Law of the Commonwealth and Chief Justice Shaw: The Evolution of American Law, 1830–1860* (1957), Leonard Levy traces these developments through the life and opinions of Lemuel Shaw, Chief Justice of the Massachusetts Supreme Court and one of the nation's most influential jurists. The chapters on the criminal law contain much valuable information on rights of the accused. Virginia's experience is discussed in Kathryn Preyer, "Crime, the Criminal Law, and Reform in Post-Revolutionary Virginia," *Law and History Review* (1985).

Recent years have witnessed several excellent studies of criminal justice in other antebellum states. Michael Hindus compares northern and southern justice in *Prison and Plantation: Crime, Justice, and Authority in Massachusetts and South Carolina, 1767–1878* (1980). An earlier study is Jack K. Williams, *Vogues in Villainy: Crime and Retribution in Ante-Bellum South Carolina* (1959). Georgia is the focus of Edward L. Ayers, *Vengeance and Justice: Crime and Punishment in the Nineteenth-Century South* (1984), while David J. Bodenhamer examines changes in criminal process and institutions, especially the grand and petit juries, in the Midwest in *The Pursuit of Justice: Crime and Law in Antebellum Indiana* (1986). Allen Steinberg, *The Transformation of Criminal Justice: Philadelphia, 1800–1880* (1989), provides a unique look at the shift from private to public prosecution in Philadelphia's lowest courts. A valuable study of the development of urban law enforcement is Roger Lane, *Policing the City: Boston, 1822–1885* (1967).

Despite their importance in the original American scheme of rights, there is a very thin body of scholarship on the legal history of juries. Richard D. Younger, *People's Panel: The Grand Jury in the United States, 1641–1941* (1963), remains the standard survey on the grand inquest. Petit juries lack even the most cursory survey. For this period, a good introduction is an unattributed law review article: "The Changing Role of the Jury in the Nineteenth Century," *Yale Law Review* (1964). Mark De Wolfe Howe, "Juries as Judges of Criminal Law," *Harvard Law Review* (1939), also contains valuable information.

Historians have paid considerably more attention to the era's practice of punishment and its implications for the "cruel and unusual" clause of the Eighth Amendment. Louis P. Masur examines the use and social meaning of the death penalty in *Rites of Execution: Capital Punishment and the Transformation of American Culture, 1776–1865* (1989), while David Brion Davis, "The Movement to Abolish Capital Punishment in America, 1787–1861," *American Historical Review* (1957), remains the best introduction to the crusade against the gallows. The establishment of the penitentiary, and the hopes and fears of its creators, is the subject of David J. Rothman, *The Discovery of the Asylum: Social Order and Disorder in the New Republic* (1971).

The procedural protections afforded slaves in criminal trials is a controversial subject among scholars. Daniel Flanigan, "Criminal Procedure in Slave Trials in the Antebellum South," *Journal of Southern History* (1974), argues that southern courts paid attention to due process guarantees, a view shared in large measure by A. E. Keir Nash, "Reason of Slavery: Understanding the Judicial Role in the Peculiar Institution," *Vanderbilt Law Review* (1979). Although scholars have challenged his interpretations, Philip J. Schwarz presents much detailed information on the cruel charade of slave justice in *Twice Condemned: Slaves and the Criminal Laws of Virginia, 1705–1865* (1988).

Chapter 4—The Meaning of Due Process, 1865–1930

Two volumes in the American Nation series serve as excellent introductions to the various constitutional and legal issues of the Reconstruction era and the late nineteenth and early twentieth centuries. Harold Hyman and William C. Wiecek, *Equal Justice Under Law: Constitutional Development, 1835–1875* (1982), offer a superb survey of the complex interaction of law and politics during the Civil War era, including the adoption of the Thirteenth, Fourteenth, and Fifteenth Amendments to the Constitution. Loren P. Beth also provides a broad focus to constitutional law in *The Development of the American Constitution, 1877–1917* (1971). Both books discuss the rights of criminal defendants in some detail. Readers will also want to consult Harold M. Hyman, *A More Perfect Union: The Impact of the Civil War and Reconstruction on the Constitution* (1975). Richard C. Cortner, *The Supreme Court and the Second Bill of Rights: The Fourteenth Amendment and the Nationalization of Civil Liberties* (1981) is indispensable on the incorporation of rights of the accused under the Fourteenth Amendment. Although it does not devote attention to criminal justice, students interested in the late nineteenth-century constitutional order at both federal and state levels should consult Morton Keller, *Affairs of State: Public Life in Late Nineteenth Century America* (1977). Changes in the role of federal judges during the period are discussed in G. Edward White, *The American Judicial Tradition: Profiles of Leading American Judges* (1976).

There is an extensive literature on the civil rights question during reconstruction and afterwards. Among the most useful are Herman Belz, *Emancipation and Equal Rights: Politics and Constitutionalism in the Civil War Era* (1978); Howard J. Graham, *Everyman's Constitution: Historical Essays on the Fourteenth Amendment, the Conspiracy Theory, and the Constitution* (1968); Robert J. Harris, *The Quest for Equality: The Constitution, Congress, and the Supreme Court* (1960); and William E. Nelson, *The Fourteenth Amendment: From Political Principle to Judicial Doctrine* (1988). Stanley I. Cutler, *Judicial Power and Reconstruction Politics* (1968), and Robert J. Kaczorowski, *The Politics of Judicial Interpretation: Federal Courts, the Department of Justice, and Civil Rights, 1866–1876* (1985), reveal the increasingly important judicial role in the creation and promotion of civil rights. The problems of enforcement are discussed in Donald G. Nieman, *To Set the Law in Motion: The Freedman's Bureau and the Legal Rights of Blacks, 1865–1868* (1979). Thomas D. Morris examines the impact of reconstruction policy on the most recalcitrant Southern state in "Equality, 'Extraordinary Law,' and Criminal Justice: The South Carolina Experience, 1865–1866," *South Carolina Historical Magazine* (1982). The failure of these and other developments to provide meaningful protection to black

Americans is the subject of Neil McMillen's powerful book, *Dark Journey: Black Mississippians in the Age of Jim Crow* (1989).

Historians have begun to address in detail the dramatic changes in criminal justice that occurred in the late nineteenth and twentieth centuries. Unquestionably the best study of the system in operation, one that discusses the changes in a single California county, is Lawrence M. Friedman and Robert V. Percival, *The Roots of Justice: Crime and Punishment in Alameda County, California, 1870–1910* (1981). Albert W. Alschuler traces the increasing use of plea bargaining as a primary tool of criminal prosecutors in "Plea Bargaining and Its History," *Columbia Law Review* (1975). Another important development was the decline of jury trial, an innovation discussed in Susan C. Towne, "The Historical Origins of Bench Trial for Serious Crimes," *American Journal of Legal History* (1979). Eric Monkkonen, *Police in Urban America, 1860–1920* (1981) discusses the response of police to the rise of the large city, while Anthony Platt, *The Child Savers: The Invention of Delinquency* (1969), traces the Progressive Era's solution for what is now called juvenile delinquency. The effect of new technologies on police practices and rights of the accused is the subject of Walter F. Murphy, *Wiretapping on Trial* (1965).

Chapter 5—Fair Trial, Federalism, and Rights of the Accused

Paul L. Murphy ably discusses constitutional developments from the end of World War I through the Kennedy-Johnson years in *The Constitution of Crisis Times, 1918–1969* (1972), a work that devotes much attention to civil liberties, including rights of criminal defendants. A more direct focus on these guarantees and their incorporation into the Fourteenth Amendment is found in Richard C. Cortner, *The Supreme Court and the Second Bill of Rights* (1981). Another good overview is Henry J. Abraham, *Freedom and the Court: Civil Rights and Liberties in the United States* (5th ed., 1988). G. Edward White, *Patterns of American Legal Thought* (1978), and John W. Johnson, *American Legal Culture, 1908–1940,* explore early twentieth-century shifts in legal thought and culture that accompanied these changes. The importance of the American Civil Liberties Union to the expansion of defendant's rights is treated in Samuel Walker, *In Defense of American Liberties: A History of the ACLU* (1989).

The clash between Justices Frankfurter and Black over the doctrine of incorporation is the subject of James F. Simon, *The Antagonists: Hugo Black, Felix Frankfurter and Civil Liberties in Modern America* (1989). Both men have been the subject of numerous judicial biographies, which is an excellent way for students to become acquainted with the conflict in philosophy and style. The best works are James J. Magee, *Mr. Justice Black: Absolutist on the Court* (1980),

Howard Ball, *The Vision and the Dream of Justice Hugo L. Black: An Examination of a Judicial Philosophy* (1975), Gerald T. Dunne, *Hugo Black and the Judicial Revolution* (1977), Clyde Jacobs, *Justice Frankfurter and Civil Liberties* (1961), H. N. Hirsch, *The Enigma of Felix Frankfurter* (1981), and Samuel J. Konefsky, *The Constitutional World of Mr. Justice Frankfurter* (1949).

Studies of landmark and other important cases offer another fruitful way to learn about rights of the accused in these transitional decades. Dan T. Carter, *Scottsboro: A Tragedy of the American South* (rev. ed., 1979), is a model of careful scholarship and well-crafted prose about a seminal case in extending protection of the Bill of Rights to defendants in state courts. An earlier case which foreshadowed the outcome of *Powell* v. *Alabama* was *Moore* v. *Dempsey* (1923), which is the subject of Richard C. Cortner, *A Mob Intent on Death: The NAACP and the Arkansas Riot Cases* (1988). Two other studies deserve mention: Charles H. Martin, *The Angelo Herndon Case and Southern Justice* (1976), examines the impact anti-communist hysteria had on due process in the 1930s, while Stephen J. Whitfield, *A Death in the Delta: The Story of Emmet Till* (1988), focuses on the breakdown of due process in the 1955 Mississippi lynching of a black teenager from Chicago.

Chapter 6—Judicial Liberalism and the Due Process Revolution

The literature on the Warren Court seems limitless. Scholars have devoted considerable attention to the various criminal law issues litigated before the Supreme Court, yet there are surprisingly few surveys of the due process revolution, at least as it affected criminal defendants. A good general introduction to the Warren Court's reform of criminal procedure remains one written at the end of the decade, Fred P. Graham, *The Due Process Revolution: The Warren Court's Impact on Criminal Law* (1970). A more recent scholarly assessment that also discusses the Court in the 1970s and 1980s is provided by Mel Urofsky, *The Continuity of Change: The Supreme Court and Individual Liberties, 1953–1986* (1989). Also, readers should again consult two works mentioned earlier, Richard C. Cortner, *The Supreme Court and the Second Bill of Rights* (1981) and Paul Murphy, *The Constitution in Crisis Times, 1918–1969* (1972).

G. Edward White, *Earl Warren: A Public Life* (1982) and Bernard Schwartz, *Super Chief: Earl Warren and His Supreme Court* (1983), are good biographies of the man and his times. Valuable accounts of the Warren Court include: Alexander M. Bickel, *The Supreme Court and the Idea of Progress* (1970); Archibald Cox, *The Warren Court: Constitutional Decision as an Instrument of Reform* (1968); Leonard W. Levy, ed., *The Supreme Court under Earl Warren* (1972); and Philip B. Kurland, *Politics, the Constitution, and the Warren Court*

(1970). The perspective of a justice who sided with the Court's liberal majority during his brief tenure is found in Arthur J. Goldberg, *Equal Justice: The Supreme Court in the Warren Era* (1971).

A dated but still valuable right-by-right survey of criminal due process that includes much information on issues before the Warren Court is David Fellman, *The Defendant's Rights Today* (1975). *New York Times'* prize-winning commentator Anthony Lewis wrote the classic account of Gideon v. Wainwright (1963), the right-to-counsel case, in *Gideon's Trumpet* (1964). Filled with details about the case in state courts and on federal appeal, the book served as the basis for a popular made-for-TV movie in the 1980s. Otis H. Stephens surveys the legal issues involved in criminal confessions in *The Supreme Court and Confessions of Guilt* (1973). For the general controversy over the law and order issues before the Court, including the impact of decisions on police practices, see V. A. Leonard, *The Police, the Judiciary, and the Criminal* (1969), and Theodore L. Becker, ed., *The Impact of Supreme Court Decisions* (1969). The Omnibus Crime Control and Safe Streets Act of 1968 is discussed in Adam C. Breckenridge, *Congress Against the Court* (1970). Stephen L. Wasby, *The Impact of the United States Supreme Court: Some Perspectives* (1970), discusses public reaction to the Court's due process decisions.

Chapter 7—Rights of the Accused in a Conservative Age

Scholarly literature on the Burger Court's decisions in criminal justice is scanty, appearing most often in law reviews. Two collections of essays, however, offer an adequate overview of the most important issues: Vincent Blasi, ed., *The Burger Court: The Counter-Revolution That Wasn't* (1983) and Herman Schwartz, ed., *The Burger Years: Rights and Wrongs in the Supreme Court, 1969–1986* (1987). Dissenting from the general interpretation that the Burger Court did not reverse Warren Court decisions on criminal due process is Leonard W. Levy, *Against the Law: The Nixon Court and Criminal Justice* (1974), although Levy wrote before the Court shifted to a more moderate stance in this area. James F. Simon, *In His Own Image: The Supreme Court in Richard Nixon's America* (1973), offers another early assessment of Richard Nixon's success in shaping the Court. The philosophy of the current Chief Justice is discussed in Sue Davis, *Justice Rehnquist and the Constitution* (1988).

Capital punishment has received considerable attention from scholars. Michael Meltsner, *Cruel and Unusual: The Supreme Court and Capital Punishment* (1973), examines the justices' often ambivalent attitude toward the death penalty. Advocating abolishment of the death penalty are Hugo Bedau, *The Courts, the Constitution, and Capital Punishment* (1977) and Charles L. Black, Jr., *Capital Punishment: The Inevitability of Caprice and Mistake* (2nd ed., 1981). A pro-capital punishment position is found in Walter Burns, *For Capital Punishment: Crime and the Morality of the Death Penalty* (1979).

Justice William Brennan's article, "State Constitutions and the Protection of Individual Rights," *Harvard Law Review* (1977), called for a revival of state protection of rights that would supersede federal guarantees, including rights of the accused. Shirley S. Abrahamson has written extensively on the subject; see, for example, "Criminal Law and State Constitutions: The Emergence of State Constitutional Law," *Texas Law Review* (1985). A less optimistic view about the possibility of meaningful state guarantees is expressed by Donald E. Wilkes, Jr., "First Things Last: Amendomania and State Bills of Rights," *Mississippi Law Journal* (1984).

INDEX OF CASES

INDEX

ACLU. *See* American Civil Liberties Union

Accused, rights of. *See also* Due process; Rights
in colonial law, 10, 15, 18–20
to confront witnesses, 119–20
and federalism, 50, 74–75
and *Miranda* warnings, 136
and police, 62–63
and the Revolution, 34, 42–43
and sociological jurisprudence, 95
and state law, 80
and U.S. Constitution, 45–47

Activism, judicial, 8, 110–11, 115–20

Adams, John, 32, 36

"Address to the Inhabitants of Quebec," 37

Alameda County (Calif.), criminal justice in, 87–88

American Civil Liberties Union (ACLU), 96–97, 116, 133

American Law Institute, 124

Antifederalists, 45

Appeal, 19, 26, 90–91

Articles of Confederation, 43–44

Assizes of Clarendon and Northhampton, 12

Attainder, bills of, 39, 44

Attorneys. *See* Counsel, right of; Lawyers

Attorneys General, state, 117, 120

Bail
antebellum, 63
in Bill of Rights, 46
in colonial law, 16, 19, 22
denial of, 136
and state constitutions, 43

Bail Reform Act (1984), 136

Bar, professional, 28, 62

Beccaria, Cesare, 42, 56

Bentham, Jeremy, 59

Bible, 10, 20

Bill of Rights (1689), 17

Bill of Rights (states), 136–37

Bill of Rights (U.S. Constitution), 16, 38, 45–47. *See also* Due process; *specific Amendments*
and due process, 5, 66, 101
and Fourteenth Amendment, 73–74, 80–82, 93–94, 99–100, 116–17
and juvenile courts, 125
nationalization of, 9, 94, 110, 113, 128
and states, 6, 50, 70–71, 73–74, 92, 93–95, 98
and Supreme Court, 111, 130

Bishop, Joel P., 5–6, 62

Black, Hugo
and Bill of Rights, 101, 111
and Fourteenth Amendment, 99, 103, 104, 108, 117

Black Codes, 72, 73

167